T0312268

Cambridge Elements

Elements in Pragmatics
edited by
Jonathan Culpeper
Lancaster University, UK
Michael Haugh
University of Queensland, Australia

PRAGMATICS, UTTERANCE MEANING, AND REPRESENTATIONAL GESTURE

Jack Wilson
University of Salford

CAMBRIDGE
UNIVERSITY PRESS

CAMBRIDGE
UNIVERSITY PRESS

Shaftesbury Road, Cambridge CB2 8EA, United Kingdom

One Liberty Plaza, 20th Floor, New York, NY 10006, USA

477 Williamstown Road, Port Melbourne, VIC 3207, Australia

314–321, 3rd Floor, Plot 3, Splendor Forum, Jasola District Centre, New Delhi – 110025, India

103 Penang Road, #05–06/07, Visioncrest Commercial, Singapore 238467

Cambridge University Press is part of Cambridge University Press & Assessment, a department of the University of Cambridge.

We share the University's mission to contribute to society through the pursuit of education, learning and research at the highest international levels of excellence.

www.cambridge.org
Information on this title: www.cambridge.org/9781009454407

DOI: 10.1017/9781009031080

First published 2024

A catalogue record for this publication is available from the British Library.

ISBN 978-1-009-45440-7 Hardback
ISBN 978-1-009-01379-6 Paperback
ISSN 2633-6464 (online)
ISSN 2633-6456 (print)

Cambridge University Press & Assessment has no responsibility for the persistence or accuracy of URLs for external or third-party internet websites referred to in this publication and does not guarantee that any content on such websites is, or will remain, accurate or appropriate.

Pragmatics, Utterance Meaning, and Representational Gesture

Elements in Pragmatics

DOI: 10.1017/9781009031080
First published online: January 2024

Jack Wilson
University of Salford

Author for correspondence: Jack Wilson, j.j.wilson@salford.ac.uk

Abstract: Humans produce utterances intentionally. Visible bodily action, or gesture, has long been acknowledged as part of the broader activity of speaking, but it is only recently that the role of gesture during utterance production and comprehension has been the focus of investigation. If we are to understand the role of gesture in communication, we must answer the following questions: Do gestures communicate? Do people produce gestures with an intention to communicate? This Element argues that the answer to both these questions is yes. Gestures are (or can be) communicative in all the ways language is. This Element arrives at this conclusion on the basis that communication involves prediction. Communicators predict the behaviours of themselves and others, and such predictions guide the production and comprehension of utterance. This Element uses evidence from experimental and neuroscientific studies to argue that people produce gestures because doing so improves such predictions.

Keywords: Inference, Gesture, Intention, Prediction, Pragmatics

ISBNs: 9781009454407 (HB), 9781009013796 (PB), 9781009031080 (OC)
ISSNs: 2633-6464 (online), 2633-6456 (print)

Contents

1 Communication, Pragmatics and Prediction

1.1 Introduction

Why are humans so good at communicating? The simple answer is that we possess languages. Languages are rich, systematic pairings of types of action with representations. The representational capacity of language is infinite. Language can be used to describe what is, what was and what might be. As a result, the communicational capacities of a language-possessing species are equally infinite. The reason I call this the simple answer is that it often leads to the idea that humans are good at communicating because of a single tool (i.e., language). Evidence for this view can be found in the lack of language in any non-human species.

The less simple answer is that humans possess a suite of *cognitive gadgets* (Heyes, 2018) that make us good at working out other people's goals, intentions, thoughts, and so on. These gadgets make humans particularly susceptible to attempts at communication. Evidence for this view can be found in the fact that linguistic acts often communicate more than their conventionally paired representations. In other words, what we *mean* is often different from what we *say*. Additional evidence for this view is that humans communicate in a range of non-linguistic ways. For example, pointing gestures are present in every documented human culture on the planet (Cooperrider, Slotta & Nunez, 2018). Further, in every documented culture, pre-linguistic infants point to communicate prior to language (Liszkowski et al., 2012). Human pointing, like other forms of human communication, involves what might be called *mind reading* (Heyes & Frith, 2014; Sperber & Wilson, 2002), which is the process of representing someone else's mental states. If I point to something, I not only want you to engage with it, I also want you to realise that I want you to engage with it. Human-like pointing, just like language, has not been observed in any non-human species (Tomasello, 2006).

Both of these answers are partly correct. It is possible to outline two capacities of importance to human communication: a *semantic capacity* for representing/presenting thoughts linguistically and a *pragmatic capacity* for working out why someone presented those thoughts linguistically. Mind reading, I believe, is a key component of this pragmatic capacity.[1] Within linguistics, the complementary fields of semantics and pragmatics have been involved in exploring the nature of these two capacities. Broadly, semantics is the study of

---

[1] As suggested by a reviewer, communicators are also capable of representing counterfactuals, imagining what other things might have happened, and use this ability to work out why something was said. I agree with this point, but would argue that mind reading plays an apparently unique role in human communication.

the rules connecting linguistic form with meaning. Pragmatics can be thought of as the study of what an utterance is taken to mean in a particular context, focussing on how features of extra-linguistic setting or environment play a role in determining why an utterance conveying a particular semantic content was presented. As a result of this focus, pragmatics can be considered narrowly to be about how the production and comprehension of a linguistic act goes beyond semantic rules or more broadly to involve exploring the interactional achievement of two or more individuals, not as separate individuals but as a complex interactional unit (H. H. Clark, 1996). Here, my focus is on the narrower construal of pragmatics, but I will touch upon the notion of joint action in Section 1.5.

Gesture studies has emerged as a discipline that explores the ways in which non-linguistic behaviours have an impact on communication. Therefore, gesture studies and pragmatics share the fundamental supposition that communication does not end with the conventional pairing of language and representation. Language is just one resource among the many that people employ during communication. The goal of this Element is to explore the relationship between gesture and pragmatics by exploring the role of gesture in linguistic communication.[2]

My main conclusion is that gestures are (or can be) communicative in all the ways language is. I arrive at this conclusion on the basis that communication involves prediction. Communicators predict the behaviours of themselves and others, and such predictions guide production and comprehension. When these predictions are accurate, things move on (guided by new predictions). However, when predictions are not accurate, resulting in prediction errors, communicators must infer novel explanations. Over time, communicators reduce such prediction errors by improving their predictions. People gesture because doing so reduces prediction errors associated with communicative acts. Describing how gestures perform a role in facilitating prediction will be the focus of Section 4. However, in this first section I will spend some time outlining a theory of communication that incorporates pragmatic theories of language and predictive theories of the mind.[3] In Section 2 I introduce gesture and outline the major theories of gesture production in both pragmatics and the

---

[2] By gesture I am referring to primarily manual representational contributions that communicators make. I do not mean to include human behaviours such as crying or blushing. I will spend Section 2 defining what I mean by gesture. Interested readers may wish to jump to that section first.

[3] In order to make this work accessible to scholars across various pragmatic disciplines and gesture studies, I do not adopt a single pragmatic theory, but conceptualise communication in a way that I hope will be acceptable to many scholars working within pragmatics.

gesture literature. In Section 3 I explore the experimental evidence for the role of gesture in communication. Finally, in Section 4 I bring everything together as a model of utterance production and comprehension that can accommodate gesture, without violating the core tenets of pragmatics.

1.2 What Is Communication?

1.2.1 Signs and Signals

Humans are not the only things on the planet that communicate. Many non-human animals and human-made systems communicate. At its heart, communication is a form of meaning making, but not all meaning is a form of communication. Since Grice (1957) it has been acknowledged that the word *meaning* is fairly vague. The terms *sign* and *signal* have been used to describe two types of meaningful phenomena, but only signals are communicative (Bara, 2010; Hauser, 1996; Wharton, 2009).[4] Some examples can help illuminate the difference.

Domesticated dogs (*canis lupus familiaris*) have olfactory capabilities that far exceed human beings (Kokocińska-Kusiak et al., 2021). For example, it has been shown that dogs can detect the presence of a rodent 50 m away (Gsell et al., 2010). In this case the scent trail left by the rodent is a sign to the dog of the rodent's presence. Other examples of signs are things like smoke which is a sign of fire, footprints, which can also be signs of the presence of an animal, and certain spots, which can be a sign of measles. These types of sign all represent an inverse causal relationship. Fire causes smoke, the presence of an animal caused the footprints and measles cause a certain type of visible spots. Only someone or something that is capable of perceiving an effect and linking it to its cause can interpret the meaning of a sign.

We can return to dogs for an example of a signal. In addition to detecting animals via scent trails, dogs also scent mark with urine to communicate with other dogs (Kokocińska-Kusiak et al., 2021). The mark communicates to dogs information about the identity, size, sex and reproductive status of the dog who left it (Cafazzo, Natoli, & Valsecchi, 2012; McGuire & Bemis, 2017; McGuire & Kable, 2012). Scent marking is a signal that communicates specific information. Other examples of signalling include the mating dances performed by certain birds, traffic lights and the waggle dance performed by bees. What unifies signals is that they invoke a signalling system into which a signal producer

---

[4] In what follows I am conflating the notions of cue and sign. Bara (2010) provides a more detailed taxonomy.

is capable of encoding a message and from which a signal comprehender is capable of decoding that message.[5]

There is a cost associated with the creation of both signs and signals (Bara, 2010). The cost associated with the creation of a sign has nothing to do with its effectiveness as a sign. The scent trail left by a potential prey animal may be a sign to a dog, but the animal that left the trail is unlikely to have done so to communicate its presence to that dog. The cost associated with a sign's meaning is borne by the animal able to comprehend it because it has to take the time and effort to interpret the sign. This is by no means a simple process for dogs (Thesen, Steen, & Doving, 1993). The cost associated with a signal, however, *is* a function from its creation (on both an evolutionary and an individual level) to its effectiveness at communicating. On an evolutionary level, scent marking is instinctual and male dogs urinate in a distinct way by cocking their leg to direct their urine on upright structures such as trees and lampposts (Hart, 1974). The dog sniffing the mark also needs to be able to discriminate the information contained in the urine. On an individual level, both signal producer and signal comprehender have to spend the time and effort to leave and interpret a mark.

This distinction can be thought of in terms of direct and derived functions (Millikan, 1984). The direct function of scent marking is to communicate something to another dog; its purpose is to exchange information. However, being meaningful to a dog is not a direct function of a scent trail left by a prey animal, yet a dog may work out on the basis of the scent trail that a prey animal is nearby. In this case, indicating the presence of an animal is a derived function of the scent trail *to the dog*. Being meaningful is a direct function of a signal, but it can only ever be the derived function of a sign.

How does this link to human communication? One of the most prevalent features of human communication is that humans employ complex communication systems we call languages. Languages are signalling systems par excellence. However, in Sections 1.2.2–1.3 I will argue that being able to interpret signs and not signals is the basis for most human communication.

1.2.2 Human Communication

What is the basis for human communication? A potential answer is that humans communicate by encoding their thoughts into signals that are communicative because someone else has access to the same signalling system. This description is a very simplified version of what has become known as the *code*

---

[5] Throughout this Element I will use the word *producer* to refer to the thing or person responsible for producing a communicative behaviour and *comprehender* for the thing or person that interprets it.

model of communication (Shannon & Weaver, 1949). Within pragmatics it has been repeatedly demonstrated that this kind of approach rarely works (Bara, 2010; Sperber & Wilson, 1995; Stenning, Lascarides & Calder, 2006; Wharton, 2009). An example[6] can show why:

(1)   tiśbūb   bark-īs   w-axayr   h-ūk   tiśbūb   aġawf
       you.climb into-it.f. and-better for-you.m.s. you.climb up
       'You climb into it and it's better for you to go up'

In (1) M1, who is a user of Mehri, an endangered modern South Arabian language, is describing how to get to a researcher's home. Just before (1) he said that he would rather take a bus than walk. In (1) he explains how he likes to sit on the upper deck of the bus. Without access to Mehri, it is impossible to understand what M1 is communicating. Examples like (1) appear to be excellent evidence that humans can communicate because two people with access to a signalling system (Mehri, in this case) can understand each other's messages. However, if we only take the signal into account then we would be missing a lot of M1's message. The context also plays a role in determining M1's message. For instance, M1 is speaking to a researcher, who is being referred to with the second-person form of 'tiśbūb' (lit. *you go up*). If this was said to someone else it would refer to a different person. So the physical setting is playing a role in determining M1's message. Also, M1 does not actually mention stairs or an upper deck in his description; this must be worked out on the basis that he has already expressed a preference for getting on the bus and with the general knowledge that buses may include things like upper decks. So general knowledge is playing a role in determining M1's message. Finally, despite the fact that his utterance is realised as an imperative, M1 is not commanding the researcher to climb into the bus and go up the stairs; rather, he is expressing a preference for doing so (which might be paraphrased as *if you get the chance you should ...*). So M1's reason for saying (1) is playing a role in determining M1's message. These three points are all part of the context used in order to understand the meaning of M1's utterance, showing that human linguistic communication goes beyond applying a signalling system.

1.2.3 Saying and Meaning

Since the work of Grice (see Grice, 1989), most scholars working on pragmatics have suggested that a communicative act can be considered in terms of *what is*

---

[6] I would like to thank Janet Watson and the local researchers from Oman for permitting me to use this example and supporting with translation and analysis.

said and *what is meant.*[7] It is possible to say that *M1 said the word 'tiśbūb'* or that *M1 said 'tiśbūb bark-īs w-axayr h-ūk tiśbūb aġawf'*, which suggests that what is said is a complete linguistic element (e.g., word or sentence). However, what M1 meant is a vaguer, less determinate thing. When we think about what M1 meant, we are drawn to his reasons for saying what he did.

Grice's work was fundamentally interested in why utterances have meaning that deviates from linguistic content. Schiffer (1972, p. 7) argued that Grice's seminal 1957 paper 'Meaning' was 'the only published attempt ever made by a philosopher or anyone else to say precisely and completely what it is for someone to mean something'. Schiffer's point captures an aspect of Grice's approach that presents an interesting opportunity for gesture scholars. Grice was interested in capturing meaning *completely*. His aim was to provide a model of when people mean things and when they do not (and not just what the words a person says mean). The starting point for Grice's theory of meaning was to distinguish between two senses of the word *mean*.

In Section 1.2.1 I argued that both signs and signals have meaning but that the direct function of a signal is to communicate something. The signs and signals discussed in Section 1.2.1 are both inherently meaningful, but there is nothing inherently meaningful about M1's utterance. Grice distinguished between natural meaning (or meaning$_N$) and non-natural meaning (or meaning$_{NN}$). Natural meaning is exemplified by signs like those outlined in Section 1.2.1. Smoke means$_N$ fire; footprints mean$_N$ an animal is nearby; certain spots mean$_N$ measles. Non-natural meaning is defined by the fact that a producer intends (or m-intends in Grice's terms) to communicate a message. Grice did not provide an analysis of signals, but following other scholars working with pragmatics (Wharton, 2009) I am treating them as communicating natural meaning since signal producers (e.g., dogs, traffic lights) do not m-intend to communicate.

Why is M1's utterance not inherently meaningful? First, Mehri is composed of largely arbitrary noises that are not produced via instinct or designed program (as is the case with most animal and program-based signalling systems). And second, what he appears to be communicating is not exhausted by the meaning of what he said. Understanding both these points involves slightly different notions of meaning$_{NN}$. Grice distinguished between *timeless* meaning$_{NN}$ and *occasion-specific* meaning$_{NN}$ (Grice, 1957, 1968). Timeless meaning$_{NN}$ refers to what a hypothetical speaker would typically mean$_{NN}$ if they said something.

---

[7] This distinction is also regularly framed as a distinction between *what is said* and *what is implicated*. However, within the pragmatics literature there are rifts about what constitutes saying and implicating. Kepa and Perry (2020) provide an excellent introduction to pragmatics and the 'near' and 'far-side' distinction.

In other words, the meaning of what was said. And occasion-specific meaning refers to what a producer actually meant.

For linguistic communication it is assumed that, unless there is evidence to the contrary, producers intend to communicate the timeless meaning$_{NN}$ of what they say. The timeless meaning$_{NN}$ of a communicative act is determined by the semantic rules of a language. However, when there is evidence to the contrary, what a producer m-intends to communicate can be very different from what they have said.

Going back to the notion of direct and derived functions, it seems that the direct function of an utterance is to say something and a derived function is to mean$_{NN}$ something. This is partially correct since a comprehender can derive meaning that goes beyond what a producer is saying. However, it also puts the cart before the horse. The difference between communicative acts and natural signals can be exemplified by an analogy (Fiengo, 2007; Kissine, 2013). The direct function of a hammer is to hit in a nail. A derived function of a hammer is to build a house. However, no one would argue that using a hammer is the reason why someone built a house. This is because the desire to build a house existed before the hammer was used and the hammer is a tool that helps achieve this desire. In the same way, it does not make sense to suggest that *what is said* is the reason for *what is meant*. The desire to communicate something is the reason a producer said anything in the first place. In other words, the content of an utterance (i.e., *what is said*) is a tool for communicating *what is meant*. From this perspective, all human communicative acts involve the inference (see Box 1) of what is meant based on the evidence of what is said (Grice, 1957; Sperber & Wilson, 1995).

Box 1 Inference

An *inference* is a conclusion reached on the basis of evidence and reasoning. However, while they can be, there is no reason to assume that inferences are consciously entertained. It is possible to argue that a dog infers the presence of another animal on the basis of a scent trail, but the inference is unlikely to be conscious. Equally, it is not necessary that the comprehender of M1's utterance is aware of the fact that they are inferring what he meant on the basis of what he said and the context. As will be discussed in Section 1.6, many cognitive processes can be analysed as being inferential.

Examples like (1) have led many working in pragmatics to think that humans are good at communicating because they are very good at inferring the reasons behind people's actions more generally. For example, upon seeing someone close a window, we might immediately jump to the conclusion that they are cold and they want to warm the room up. Using the definitions of signs and signals, a person's action is a sign of the reason a person has for performing that action. It is a natural sign of their intention. However, unlike instrumental actions and scent trails (see Section 1.2.1), which are *natural signs*, communicative behaviours are produced with an awareness of what effect they might have. Such an awareness plays a role in why a certain communicative behaviour was produced. Communicative behaviours are *non-natural signs*. So what does this mean for the status of language? While it is possible to infer intentions from acts, it is not really possible to infer complex representational contents from acts. To borrow an example from Sperber and Wilson (1995), it might be possible to infer that someone wants you to fix or replace their hairdryer from the fact that they have left a broken one in a place where you are likely to see it. However, as the complexity of what a producer wants to communicate increases, so too does the necessity of a linguistic or similarly complex system. From this perspective, language is a system that conventionally pairs linguistic form with meaning (H. H. Clark, 1996; Lewis, 1969). In other words, language is a shortcut to a lengthy inferential process of working out what someone is thinking (Enfield, 2009; Sperber, 1995). Language is a non-natural signalling system that makes interpreting the non-natural signs of communicators much easier. However, because the main business of communication is inferring non-natural signs, it is possible to infer much more than is dictated by the signalling system. Humans can use signals to communicate beyond their associated meanings. Box 2 presents a taxonomy of signs and signals using the notion of natural and non-natural meaning.

Box 2 Natural and Non-natural Signs and Signals

Natural Sign	**Natural Signal**
The scent left by a rodent is a natural sign of the rodent's presence.	Canine scent marking is a natural signal communicating the size, sex and so on of the dog that left the scent.
Non-natural Sign	**Non-natural Signal**
Leaving a broken hairdryer in a place where someone is likely to see it is a non-natural sign that the person who left it wants the person who found it to repair it.	An utterance of *Would you fix my broken hairdryer?* is a non-natural signal of the fact that the producer wants their interlocutor to fix their hairdryer.

1.2.4 Specifying Context

Even if we accept that a person can work out what someone means based on what they have said and that their message is not exhausted by the contents of their utterance, we still need to explain how people do this. What information does an utterance producer use to design their utterances and what information does a comprehender use to interpret them? The general answer is that people use context. However, context has been a debated topic within the pragmatics literature and in this section I will briefly outline four assumptions that are involved in the inference of what is meant from what is said.

The first assumption is that producers are (at least partially) rational (Grice, 1975). If we assume that a producer (P) had a range of behaviours, $\{b_1, b_2, \ldots, b_n\}$, to choose from, then P has picked the best behaviour to communicate their message, taking into account how costly it was to produce that behaviour. This cost–benefit equation results in the behaviour with the highest utility (Goodman & Frank, 2016; Lewis, 1969; Parikh, 2019). So information about what a producer could have done but has not may play a role in interpreting what they mean. I will have more to say about utility in Section 1.5, but the intuitive idea will do for now.

The second assumption is that humans have prosocial motivations (Heyes, 2018). However, this does not mean that people are always helpful; it is often enough that humans accommodate other people and share goals with them. Typically, communication is embedded within a non-communicative activity (e.g., cooking together) and an utterance is interpreted to the extent that it contributes to that activity (Bara, 2010; H. H. Clark, 1996; Levinson, 1979).

The third assumption is that people share a lot of knowledge or common ground (H. H. Clark, 1996; Lewis, 1969; Stalnaker, 2002). For communication, a language is a big part of common ground, but communicators also typically share knowledge about cultures and institutions. Common ground can also refer to personal knowledge that may lead to an understanding of what an utterance producer means. Communicators also share a spatial setting, which has been referred to as visual common ground (Rubio-Fernández, 2019).

The fourth assumption is that communicators are capable of metarepresenting other people's cognitive states (e.g., intentions) (Sperber & Wilson, 1995). Intention reading plays a fundamental role in many post-Gricean models of communication. For this reason I will spend the next section outlining what I mean by intention.

1.2.5 A Closer Look at Intention

Before going further, I want to specify what I mean by *intention*. One definition (see Davidson, 2001; Kockelman, 2012) is that intentions are inferences. This is represented in Box 3.

Box 3 Inferences in Intentions	
Premise 1:	If I close the window, the room will warm.
Premise 2:	I want the room to warm.
Conclusion:	So I shall close the window.

In Box 3, Premise 1 is a belief of a causal relationship between two things. Premise 2 is a pro-attitude. Taken together, Premises 1 and 2 are the *conditions of satisfaction* of the intention (Searle, 1983). The conclusion is the action plan that will satisfy Premises 1 and 2. If someone was asked to provide a reason why they closed a window, they could provide both Premise 1 and Premise 2 as reasons.

This way of thinking about intentions sometimes leads to the assumption that people should be conscious of their intentions (Bara, 2010, p. 78). I do not think this is necessarily the case, but will hold off on an explanation for now. There is also no need to suggest that the type of causal statement represented in Premise 1 need be a *belief* at all; it could be a learnt association (see Heyes, 2018) which the intender is not even aware they hold.

1.2.6 Defining Communicative Acts

Taking inference and intention into consideration, Box 4 presents a Gricean definition of communicative acts. This definition follows a contemporary Gricean approach to communicative acts (Bara, 2010; Moore, 2017; Neale, 1992; Sperber & Wilson, 1995).

Box 4 Definition of a Communicative Act
Within a particular context U, a behaviour B is a non-natural sign of a message M if:
1. the producer P of B intends to communicate M;
2. P intends condition (1) to be inferable by a comprehender C.

The definition in Box 4 has two parts. The first is that the producer intended for a behaviour to communicate a particular message. The second says that the producer intends condition (1) to be inferable by a comprehender.

This characterisation of communication is often referred to as *ostensive* (Sperber & Wilson, 1995). For example, Tomasello (2010) has adopted the same analysis for understanding the meaning of pointing gestures, but it can be applied to any communicative behaviour (Sperber & Wilson, 1995). Within the pragmatics literature, conditions (1) and (2) from Box 4 are often referred to as the *informative* and the *communicative intention*, respectively (Sperber & Wilson, 1995). I will follow this convention here.

The definition of communicative acts in Box 4 represents a third-person perspective. However, it is important to represent such acts from the utterance producer's and the comprehender's perspectives. Utterance producers make practical inferences (Kenny, 1966) from intentions to actions and comprehenders make inferences to the best explanation (Harman, 1965) from action to intention. We can represent this using a similar inference to the one in Box 3, so long as we make a small adjustment. Since utterances are context-dependent, this must be represented in the syllogism in Box 5:

Box 5 Producer's Inference
Premise 1:   If I perform a behaviour B in a context U, then I will communicate M.

Premise 2:   I want to communicate M in U.

Conclusion: So I shall perform B.

The inference in Box 5 can be remodelled to explain comprehension in Box 6:

Box 6 Comprehender's Inference
Premise 1:   If I perform a behaviour B in a context U, then I will communicate M.

Premise 2: P performed B in U.

Conclusion: P wanted to communicate M.

Both producer and comprehender share the association of a behaviour B with the same message M. For the comprehender, unlike the producer, they experience the behaviour B and must work out what it is intended to communicate, namely M. In essence, the two inferential processes involve the same ingredients but in a different order. This might seem as though I am suggesting that an interpreter is working out a premise from a conclusion. As pointed out by Levinson (1995), we should not treat interpretation as 'upside down' practical reasoning where the interpreter works out on the basis of the conclusion of practical reasoning what the premise was.[8] To demonstrate this point, Levinson (1995, p. 231) argues that even though it is possible to conclude 'p' from 'p and q', this does not mean that from 'p' you could conclude 'p and q'. The reason for this is that there are no logical grounds for the validity of this second inference that would not also allow us to conclude 'p and r' or 'p and s' and so on from 'p'. Levinson (1995, p. 231) goes on to say: 'Simple though the point is, it establishes a fundamental asymmetry between actor-based accounts and interpreter-based accounts, between acting and understanding others' actions. There simply cannot be any computational solution to this problem, as so far described.'

I would argue that as I have presented things in Boxes 5 and 6, I have not fallen into this trap. My point is not that a comprehender makes an inference from a conclusion to a premise. A comprehender takes an observed action as a premise and concludes an intentional state that would make sense of the action. The comprehender is able to do this because they have access to a generalisation (what I label as Premise 1 for both utterance producer and comprehender) that a particular behaviour will communicate a particular message in the utterance context. In other words, using Levinson's example, it would be possible to conclude 'p and q' from 'p' if I have a general assumption that *if 'p' then 'p and q'*. I believe that the general question we need to answer is not directly about the difference between acting and interpreting but about why the producer and the comprehender have as a premise something that can be represented as the conditional 'if *B* then *M*'. I discussed a partial answer in Section 1.2.4. Both producers and comprehenders assume (partial) rationality, pro-social motivations and common ground. The other thing both producers and comprehenders assume is the intentional status of the other. This final point is often fairly contentious in the pragmatics literature, so I will spend the next section presenting some neurological evidence for it.

1.3 A Closer Look at the Human Capacities for Communication

At this point it should be clear that language and communication are distinct phenomena. This distinction is corroborated by neurological evidence that language and communication are related to separate networks in the brain (Noordzij et al., 2009) and the network responsible for language does not underlie the network responsible for communication (Willems & Varley, 2010). In other words, communication involves language but is not determined by it. In

---

[8] I would like to thank Michael Haugh for drawing my attention to this interpretation and to Levinson (1995).

this section, in order to explore the dissociation between language and communication further, I will explore how the capacity to interpret other people's intentions is realised neurologically.

So far I have assumed without much evidence that understanding other people during communication is fundamentally about inferring intentions. This process is often referred to as *mind reading* (Heyes & Frith, 2014; Sperber & Wilson, 1995) and involves the metarepresentation of someone else's mental states. Within pragmatics, mind reading is often treated as a single process, that involves the explicit representation of an informative intention. Critics of this approach argue that this results in a conceptualisation of communication that is overly intellectual (see Gallagher, 2020; Geurts, 2019). In this section, I argue that what is commonly referred to as mind reading is actually related to two cognitive processes, and that these two processes are realised in different neurological regions.

While bodies are observable, minds are not. However, the reasons typically given for actions are to do with mental and not physical states. For example, most people observing someone suddenly stand up are likely to attribute an intentional reason (e.g., they *want* to go somewhere) rather than a physical one (e.g., their legs *caused* them to stand). In other words, humans typically provide reasons for actions that are not visible and have the potential to be wrong.

There are at least two distinct theories (and many in between) about how mind reading works. The first theory, which developed from the discovery of mirror neurons (di Pellegrino et al., 1992; Rizzolatti & Arbib, 1998), suggests that humans are able to interpret the behaviour of others because they are able to *mirror* the neural activation that would be involved in producing a behaviour while inhibiting the action that would follow. The neural network involved in mirroring is the putative Mirror Neuron System (pMNS), which includes the anterior intraparietal sulcus (aIPS) and the premotor cortex (PMC) (Van Overwalle & Baetens, 2009). The second theory suggests that we are able to understand the behaviours of others because we can represent a model of their minds (e.g., intentions, desires, etc.) and infer based on this model why they are performing some action. The ability to represent mental states is often referred to as *mentalising*. The neural network associated with mentalising involves the precuneus (PC), the temporal parietal junction (TPJ) and the medial prefontal cortex (mPFC) (Van Overwalle & Baetens, 2009). For the rest of this Element I will refer to these areas as the mirror and the mentalising areas.

I do not want to engage in the theoretical debates associated with mentalising and mirroring (for an overview of the literature on mentalising and mirroring see Gallagher, 2020). Instead, I will follow Heyes and Frith (2014) who argue that both processes are likely to be involved in mind reading. Studies have demonstrated that these areas are activated when people are asked to consider *why* someone did something vs *how* they did it or *what* they did (Spunt, Kemmerer, & Adolphs, 2016; Spunt, Satpute, & Lieberman, 2011). The mirroring area is active during responses to all questions, but as the requirement for considering intentional states increases, so too does the involvement of the mentalising area. These findings suggests that the mirror area contributes to low-level processing of observed action and the mentalising area responds to high-level processing of mental states (Heyes & Catmur, 2020).

The identification of distinct neural areas associated with mirroring and mentalising is critical for pragmatic research because it is possible to investigate whether mental states are used to interpret what someone means. The dissociation between the mirroring and the mentalising areas has been shown to play a role in understanding communicative behaviours (Bara, Enrici, & Adenzato, 2016; Enrici et al., 2011; Enrici, Bara, & Adenzato, 2019; Noordzij et al., 2009; Willems & Varley, 2010). As a result, researchers working in pragmatics argue that a third network (which includes both the mirroring and the mentalising areas) is involved in understanding communicative intentions (Bara et al., 2016). This network, called the *Intentional Processing Network* (IPN), is modulated by the communicative nature of a behaviour. I will have more to say about this in Sections 3.2 and 3.3 when we explore the neuroscientific evidence for the communicative nature of gesture, but for now it is enough to argue that both mirroring and mentalising play a role in understanding both instrumental and communicative actions. What this means is that what is commonly referred to as mind reading may operate differently in different situations and that mentalising might come into play when understanding the intentional motivation for an act is needed, but may not when it is not.

This section has argued that actions (including communicative acts) are neurologically complex. In the next section I want to capture some of this neurological complexity theoretically.

1.4 Action

So far I have been discussing the representational function of communication. However, it is also possible to analyse communication as an instrumental phenomenon. Speech act theory is an area of pragmatic research with a focus on the instrumental nature of communicative acts (Austin, 1962; Searle, 1969). If we are to capitalise on the neuroscientific insights of the role of mirroring and mentalising in communication, it is necessary to start with an analysis of action more broadly before considering communicative acts.

Representations are not necessarily bound to the time of speaking. However, actions are bound to the time of acting. The basic theoretical unit for many conceptualisations of time are instants (t), which are points in time. Instants do not play much of a role in human conceptions of time and it is typical to think of time not as a sequence of instants but as intervals (I) that are bound by two instants (e.g., the interval between 3pm and 4pm). Following Davidson (2001), intervals can be categorised as events. In this section I build on Kissine's (2013) treatment of several important observations fundamental to speech acts.

The event (e_1) in which A raises their arm during an interval (I_1) bounded by two instants t_1 and t_2 can be represented as:

(2) $\{t_1 < t_2\}_{I1} = raised\_arm(A, e_1)$

Example (2) says that the interval, I_1, bounded by the instants, t_1 and t_2, is equivalent to the event in which A raised their arm. However, it is also possible that A's act of raising their arm may have constituted an act of voting, represented in (3):

(3) $\{t_1 < t_2\}_{I1} = vote(A, e_1)$

The point is that one event e_1 is referred to in (2) and (3), but it is conceptualised as two different actions. If we assume that A raised their arm in order to vote, then the act of raising their arm caused the act of voting. In this way, it is possible to argue that both acts are governed by the same intention, but that (3) is governed by a secondary embedded intention. Searle (1983) distinguished between these two intentions by calling the intention to vote a *prior intention* and the intention to raise their arm an *intention-in-action*. In this way we can argue that A voted *by way of* raising their arm (Searle, 2010). When Searle uses the term prior intention, he seems to be referring to consciously held plans. For example, someone could form a prior intention to vote days or weeks before the voting takes place. This is reflected in Gallagher (2020) who uses the term distal intention to talk about prior intentions. Although I think what I am presenting is compatible with Searle's and Gallagher's views, the way I use prior intention is as an intention that guides an intention-in-action where the intention-in-action guides bodily movement. Gallagher (2020) actually introduces a third intention, which he calls the motor intention. In many ways, the distinction between prior intention and intention-in-action is based on the analyst's perspective rather than the actor's. We could continue to add complexity or remove complexity and present a fairly idealised model. In what follows I aim to make the picture as complex as is necessary and no more.

It is also possible for two events to be linked by a single act. The classic example is the link between Gavrilo Princip (GP) pulling the trigger of a gun and in doing so killing Archduke Ferdinand (AF). In this example, one event

(e_1) containing the act of pulling the trigger causes another event (e_2) in which Ferdinand died.

(4) $\{t_1 < t_2\}_{I1} = pull\_the\_trigger(GP, e_1)$

(5) $\{t_3 < t_4\}_{I2} = die(AF, e_2)$

The details in (4) and (5) can be used to analyse the sentence of *Princip killed Ferdinand* as (6):

(6) $\{t_1 < t_4\}_I = cause(e_1, e_2)$

If we assume that Princip intended to kill Ferdinand then, according to Searle (2010), Princip caused Ferdinand to die *by means of* pulling the trigger. In this case, Princip had a prior intention for Ferdinand to die and he achieved it via his intention-in-action of pulling the trigger.

One complexity not discussed by Kissine is that an act at one level may be made up of multiple acts at another level.[9] This can be evidenced in the distinction between the several senses of *clap*. The generic sense of *clap₁* is that it is the bringing together of two things (e.g., hands). However, the sentence *A clapped* is not likely to refer to A bringing their hands together once, but repeatedly over a temporal interval. This sense of *clap₂* is represented in (7):

(7)   *A clapped₂*

        $\{t_1 < t_2\}_I = clap_2(A, e_1)$

        $\{t_1 < t_2\}_I = \{clap_1(A, e_{1.1}) < clap_1(A, e_{1.2}) < clap_1(A, e_{1.3})\}$

In (7), the event in which *A clapped₂* is represented as involving the sequentially produced sub-events in which *A clapped₁*. Each sub-event satisfies a separate intention-in-action, but all are satisfying a single prior intention.

It is also possible to represent every event of *A clapped₁* as involving two simultaneous actions, one of the left hand being brought into contact with the right (LH) and one of the right hand being brought into contact with the left (RH). If these two actions are not coordinated then A will fail to clap. This is represented in (8).

(8)   *A clapped₁*

        $\{t_1 < t_2\}_I = clap_1(A, e_{1.1})$

        $\{t_1 < t_2\}_I = clap_3(LH, e_{1.1}) \wedge clap_3(RH, e_{1.1})$

---

[9] Such actions have been called semelfactives in the semantics literature (Talmy, 1985).

To summarise, a single prior intention may be used to conceptualise one event as involving two actions. For example, I may vote by way of raising my arm. Equally, two events may be linked by a single prior intention. For example, GP's prior intention to kill AF was achieved by means of an intention-in-action to pull the trigger of a gun. Finally, at a different level one event may be made up of sequential and/or simultaneous sub-events. In this case, these sub-events satisfy further intentions-in-action. For example, imagine that A had a prior intention to demonstrate how much they enjoyed a performance. This prior intention is satisfied by clapping$_2$ that is made up of individual sequential acts of clapping$_1$, which are themselves made up of the simultaneous acts of the left and the right hands.

Returning to the discussion of mirroring and mentalising from Section 1.3, intentions-in-action guide bodily movement and the mirroring areas are involved in the processing of low-level intentions-in-action whereas the mentalising areas are involved in processing the higher-level prior intentions. For example, mirroring may represent the neural network associated with the intention-in-actions directly satisfied by the bodily actions of raising an arm, pulling a trigger or bringing the hands together. Mentalising, on the other hand, would involve representations of the reasons behind raising an arm, pulling a trigger or clapping in the form of metarepresented prior intentions. In the next section I will apply these ideas to communicative acts.

1.5 Communicative Acts

Since communicative acts are *acts*, the same categories of prior intention and intention-in-action can be applied to them. Within pragmatics there is a tradition of modelling communicative acts as a sequence of constituent acts at different levels (see, for example, Bara, 2010; Clark, 1996; Enfield & Sidnell, 2017; Kissine, 2013; Parikh, 2019). This tradition dates back at least to Austin's (1962) pioneering work on *speech acts* where communicative acts are divided into the following (as schematized by Enfield and Sidnell, 2017, pp. 101–2):[10]

I. Phonetic act = 'uttering certain noises'
II. Phatic act = 'uttering certain words' by means of a phonetic act
III. Rhetic act = using a phatic act 'with a sense and reference'

A. Locutionary act = rhetic act directed at someone (I–III taken together)
B. Illocutionary act = 'in what way we are using the locution'

---

[10] The quotations that appear in Enfield and Sidnell's (2017) schema are taken from Austin (1962, pp. 94–103).

C. Perlocutionary act = 'produce certain consequential effects' by means of an illocutionary act.

Following several theories within pragmatics (Schiffer, 1972; Sperber & Wilson, 1995), the relationship between locutionary act and illocutionary act can be explained using the Gricean model outlined in Section 1.2.2. The locutionary act is an act of saying something and the illocutionary act is an act of meaning something. Phrased a different way, the informative intention is satisfied by an illocutionary act and the communicative intention is satisfied by a locutionary act. A perlocutionary act satisfies what might be called a *social intention* (Bara, 2017; Tomasello, 2010). The informative intention and the social intention are sometimes treated as synonyms. However, it makes sense to distinguish them. An informative intention is an intention to inform someone of something (its conditions of satisfaction are representational) and a social intention is an intention for a comprehender to do something (its conditions of satisfaction are instrumental).

Herbert H. Clark (1996, p. 222) develops Austin's model by considering the acts of both the producer and the comprehender under a single theoretical structure he calls an *action ladder* (see Figure 1).

In the action ladder, Clark has reduced Austin's phonetic, phatic and rhetic acts to a single act of *executing*. However, by providing the responsive actions of the comprehender, Clark's model presents additional details on how the processes of production and comprehension work. The central idea of the action ladder is that the different levels are *upwardly causal* and therefore higher levels provide *downward evidence* that lower levels have been completed (Clark, 1996, pp. 147–8).

Joint projects form the top level of the action ladder. For Clark (1996), joint projects necessarily include two events in sequence, where the second event in a joint project is achieved by means of the first. For example (p. 150), a joint project may comprise A saying *please sit down* to B followed by B sitting down. Both A's and B's behaviours are considered necessary parts of the joint project.

Level	Producer A's actions	Comprehender B's actions
4	A is *proposing* joint project w to B	B is *considering* A's proposal of w
3	A is *signaling* that p for B	B is *recognizing* that p from A
2	A is *presenting* signal s to B	B is *identifying* signal s from A
1	A is *executing* behavior t for B	B is *attending* to behavior t from A

Figure 1 Action ladder (from Clark, 1996, p. 222)

	A Event			B Event
Perlocutionary	$(\{$A made B sit down		$\}_{e1}$	$\rightarrow \{$B sat down$\}_{e7})$
Illocutionary	$\{$A told B to sit down		$\}_{e1}$	$\rightarrow\{$recognising$\}_{e6}$
Locutionary	$\{$A said 'sit down' to B		$\}_{e1}$	$\rightarrow\{$identifying$\}_{e5}$
Grammatical	$\{[$sit$[$down$]_{advp}]_{vp}$		$\}_{e1}$	$\rightarrow\{$parsing$\}_{e4}$
Lexical	$\{$'sit' $\quad \}_{e1.1}$	$\{$'down' $\quad\}_{e1.2}$		$\rightarrow\{$retrieving$\}_{e3}$
Phonetic	/s/ /ɪ/ /t/ /d/ /aʊ/ /n/			
	$\{\}_e^{1.1.1} \{\}_e^{1.1.2} \{\}_e^{1.1.3} \{\}_e^{1.2.1} \{\}_e^{1.2.2} \{\}_e^{1.2.3} \rightarrow \{$hearing$\}_{e2}$			

Figure 2 Levels of action

Figure 2 combines the approaches of Austin, Kissine and Clark, together with the idea of embedded sequential acts, by considering speech acts in time. I have also replaced Austin's terms *rhetic* and *phatic* with *grammatical* and *lexical*, respectively. Figure 2 presents an analysis of the command of *sit down*.

In Figure 2 the same event is represented from a grammatical, a locutionary and an illocutionary perspective. In other words, the producer of *sit down* could be considered to have produced the sentence of English: [sit[down]$_{advp}$]$_{vp}$, said *sit down* to B and told *B to sit down*. Furthermore, the grammatical act of producing the English sentence [sit[down]$_{advp}$]$_{vp}$ is composed of the lexical acts of producing the lexeme *sit* followed by the lexeme *down*. The acts of producing lexical items are not usually taken as acts/events by themselves but are sub-events (like individual instances of clapping$_1$ in order to applaud something). If we conceptualise a grammatical act as occurring in an interval of time, the interval containing the lexical act of producing *sit* must occur prior to the interval containing the lexical act *down*. In a similar way, the lexical act of producing *sit* is made up of the phonetic acts of producing the sounds /s/, /ɪ/ and /t/.[11] The interval that includes /s/ must occur prior to the interval that includes /ɪ/. This may seem unnecessarily complex, but it will play a critical role in Section 1.6. These points can be summarised as follows: an illocutionary act is produced by way of a locutionary act that is produced by way of a grammatical act that is produced by way of multiple sequentially produced lexical acts that were produced by way of multiple sequentially produced phonetic acts.

Perlocutionary acts are joint projects and therefore they necessarily include two acts, one of the producer and one of the comprehender. These acts occur in different events. The second event is achieved by means of the first and is often referred to as a perlocutionary effect (Kissine, 2013). In general, if A has satisfied their social intention of getting B to sit down, then this entails that B

---

[11] Due to space, the braces around each phonetic appear on the line beneath the acts. So in Figure 2 '$e_{1.1.1}$' contains '/s/'.

sat down. This is identical to the Gavrilo Princip example. The perlocutionary act can be represented as:

(9) $told\_B\_to\_sit\_down(A, e_1)$

   $sit\_down(B, e_7)$

   $cause(e_1, e_7)$

If B sits down then this provides downward evidence that B *recognised* A's illocutionary act, *identified* A's locutionary act, *parsed* A's grammatical act, *retrieved* the concepts associated with A's lexical act and *heard* A's phonetic act. Following Kissine (2013), it is also possible to conceptualise each of these as a separate event. Events 2–7 are caused by means of the corresponding acts of A. However, unlike a perlocutionary act, A has still achieved their illocutionary act of telling B to sit down even if B does not sit down. However, A cannot achieve their illocutionary act if B has not identified A's locutionary act. So the event of B caused by means of the phonetic act is a requirement of A satisfying their lexical act, and the event of B caused by means of their lexical act is a requirement of A satisfying their grammatical act and so on. In the next section I will explore the ideas discussed so far using predictive models of perception and action.

1.6 Utterances and Prediction

1.6.1 Prediction

In Sections 1.2.2–1.2.4 the inferential processes involved in utterances and actions were described as if the first premises are fixed in advance. The examples of first premises included things like:

(10)   If I close the window, then the room will warm.

(11)   If I perform a behaviour B in a context U, then I will communicate M.

However, it is possible that the room will not warm or that B will not communicate M. Therefore, instead of being fixed, we should think of such conditional premises as being based on predictions. We can rewrite (10) and (11) to reflect this as:

(12)   I predict that if I close the window, then the room will warm.

(13)   I predict that if I produce an utterance B in U, then I will communicate M.

In Section 1.2.4 I said that it is typically assumed that utterance producers are partially rational and that they select their communicative act from a set of behaviours $\{b_1, b_2, \ldots, b_n\}$. If a producer picked b_1 and not b_2 then it is because b_1 had the highest utility, which means that it does the best job of communicating M while costing the least effort. Recent approaches in computational pragmatics have started to present formalisations of the types of inferential approach needed to deal with (13) (see Degen et al., 2020; Goodman & Frank, 2016). However, most approaches to the predictions involved in utterance production follow the Neo-Gricean tradition of representing a producer's choice as relating to the quantity of information in an utterance compared to alternative utterances (see Horn, 2004). For example, imagine B walks into A's office and A is sat behind their desk with a chair in front of the desk. Then A wants B to sit in the chair. In Figure 2 A said *sit down*, but there is a range of possible alternatives they could have produced:

(14) sit down

(15) B, sit down

(16) sit down on the chair

(17) B, sit down on the chair

Compared to (14), (15) and (16), both provide more-specific information. Arguably, this information would be redundant in the context just described. Alternative (17) would be even worse because it contains two pieces of unnecessary information. Contemporary pragmatics treats utterance production as an inference related to the amount of information presented against the amount of effort required to produce that information. Producers who include overly specific information are seen as presenting redundant information that is not tailored for an audience. Following Rubio-Fernández (2016, 2019), I believe this approach to be wrong. While packaging information in a utility-maximising way is an important aspect of speaking, it cannot be the inferential process driving utterance production. There is a wealth of evidence that shows that producers produce utterances that are redundant in the way just described (see Davies & Richardson, 2021, for a review).

Recall the analogy of using a hammer to build a house. Treating the prediction involved in utterance production as one relating to the quantity of information to be expressed presupposes that language has been selected as the tool to communicate a producer's message. This is the equivalent of asking *How should I use this hammer?* rather than *Which tool should I use?* This point may not play much of a role in a model of communication where a producer chooses between alternative ways of saying the same thing, but this model does not reflect the natural setting in which producers find themselves. As I will argue repeatedly throughout the rest of this Element, language is just one tool that producers use to communicate, and therefore the inference a producer makes potentially involves a range of communicative behaviours. It is for this reason that in this section I start with an exploration of predictive coding models (PCMs) of perception/cognition more generally and then reintroduce communication.

To begin then, PCMs of perception/cognition (A. Clark, 2015; Hohwy, 2013) are based on the idea that perception (including exteroception, proprioception and interoception) involves an inference from expectation to actuality. When humans perceive the world, they are not perceiving it *bottom up* like an old-fashioned video camera capturing light and via a chemical reaction leaving an image on cellulose. As countless visual illusions have shown, human beings use context-dependent *top-down* predictions to make the process of perceiving more efficient. What illusions reveal is that the perceptual process is hierarchical and based on levels representing space and time.

A good example of this process can be exemplified using the following from Clark (2015).

Depending on the reading direction, horizontal or vertical, the middle item in Figure 3 is interpreted as the number *13* or the letter *B*. This is because we are able to represent higher-level models of sequences (numbers or letters) and the sequence we are representing will be determined by whether we have just read the number *12* or the letter *A*. If I am using the number sequence model, then I predict that the next item will be a number so I perceive a number. If I am using the letter sequence model, then I predict that the next item will be a letter

Figure 3 Contextual cues set up expectations (based on Clark, 2015)

so I perceive a letter. When this prediction is accurate, we do not wait to think about what else it might have been. However, such predictions are not always accurate. For example, imagine walking down a corridor and seeing the first two horizontal digits in Figure 3 on a door, interpreting the room number as *1213*. In this case we might predict that the number on the next door would be *1214*. However, what we see is that the number on the next door is *12 C*. Seeing *12 C* creates a prediction error, not just at the level of the order of the rooms but also retrospectively in terms of the perception of the number on the room we now know to be room *12 B*. Such prediction errors may bring to consciousness processes we were not conscious of (e.g., how we had interpreted the number on the door). What this example illustrates is that predictions make perception incredibly efficient, but they might be wrong. When predictions are wrong, they result in prediction errors that help make future predictions more accurate. In the corridor example, the prediction error may result in the establishment of a model of that particular corridor that includes it having room labels consisting of the number *12* followed by a letter. This *corridor model* will mean that we no longer have to concern ourselves with whether or not the label on a door is *12 B* or *1213*, because *12 B* is directly predicted by the model.

And PCMs are also thought to be involved in human action. Prediction is used to plan actions and interpret other people's. Starting with self actions, imagine walking over to a window because you wanted to close it. In this example, temporally higher-level plans and intentions are unpacked into lower-level predictions regarding visual perception and proprioception. Our predictions relate to things including the distance between you and the window, what the window's handle will feel like, where your hand will need to be. Now imagine the alternative scenario where A is observing B closing the window; the idea is that B's behaviour can be interpreted by mirroring the predictions A would have had in that scenario and inferring their intentions, perhaps supported by mentalising and a representation of context (this was discussed in terms of intentions in Section 1.3). In other words, the same cognitive mechanism controls my behaviour and is used to interpret the behaviour of another.

If the same mechanism is involved in producing and interpreting actions, then how do I distinguish my behaviour from someone else's? The argument from Clark (2015) is that we do this by varying the precision weighting of our predictions. Precision weighting relates to how flexible our predictions are. Lower-precision-weighted predictions will not trigger a prediction error in a wider variety of situations than higher-weighted ones. When we are performing an action, the precision weighting is high because we are able to predict, with a fairly low degree of error, the future state of the perceptual system. When we are observing another, there needs to be more room for error and the precision weighting is low. The difference in precision weighting is one of the ingredients in our sense of agency. The predictions we make about our own actions are also believed to be a kind of self-fulfilling prophecy in that the way we act is driven by the predictions we make. The whole process of inferring future states of the perceptual system is referred to as *active inference* and it represents a rather neat perspective on perception and action, capturing the distinction between self, other, action and perception using the precision of predictions.

Another insight of PCMs is that when predictions are accurate, there is no need to consciously attend to lower-level processes. This is true of both perception and action. For example, when opening a window, if the handle feels the way we expect, then we are probably not aware of how tightly we have grasped it. However, we might have forgotten that we were wearing gloves and thus failed to predict the correct pressure. In this scenario there would be a prediction error related to the pressure applied to the handle that might then lead to conscious awareness of the amount of pressure we need to apply to deal with this new variable (i.e., wearing gloves).

1.6.2 Predicting Communication

Mapping PCMs onto communication appears in a range of papers by Pickering and Garrod (2007, 2013; see also Garrod & Pickering, 2004; Pickering & Gambi, 2018). Pickering and Garrod (2013) argue that the classic distinction between a producer and a comprehender who perform different actions during communication is incorrect. Instead we should distinguish between production and comprehension processes. Pickering and Garrod (2013) argue that people represent linguistic information at different levels (message, semantics, syntax, phonology, sound). These levels are hierarchical so that a higher level can be used to predict the levels beneath it. Pickering and Garrod (2013) argue that in the same way that active inference is used to make predictions from higher to lower levels during perception and action, predictions are made from higher to lower levels during utterance production and comprehension. From this perspective, the production process is a mapping from higher to lower-level representations and the comprehension process uses a mirror of this process to predict what is being communicated. An accurate prediction at a higher level (e.g., the message) reduces the necessity of consciously entertaining a prediction at a lower level (e.g., syntax) and explains why much communication is below the level of awareness.

It is possible to draw a parallel between Pickering and Garrod's levels of representation and the phonetic, lexical, grammatical, locutionary and illocutionary levels outlined earlier. If we return to the example discussed in Figure 2 where A tells B to sit down, the point of the analysis was that the same event (e_1) can be represented on multiple levels. It is possible to enrich this analysis by incorporating prediction. However, using the notions of mirroring and mentalising, we can suggest two distinct predictive pathways.

Imagine that B does not know A and B has no prior awareness of what A is going to say. Assuming that a knowledge of the English language is part of the context, then the only perceptual evidence B has for what A is saying is the first sound they produce. When considered temporally, the phonetic act of saying /sɪt daʊn/ occurs over a temporal interval where /s/ occurs before /ɪ/ and /ɪ/ occurs before /t/, and so on. In order to capture this in Figure 2, the event of producing /s/ was represented as the sub-event $e_{1.1.1}$. Upon hearing /s/, a comprehender will be predicting the upcoming sounds in the sequence. This type of prediction is a lateral prediction since it is a prediction on one level. However, lateral predictions are supported by awareness of higher levels (e.g., that the language, S, is English). If an utterance starts with the phonetic act /s/ ($e_{1.1.1}$) then the lexical act ($e_{1.1}$) must be a word that begins with /s/ and the grammatical act must begin with a lexical act beginning /s/. Imagine that the comprehender predicts that A is performing the lexical act *sit* at $e_{1.1}$. Predicting that the lexical act $e_{1.1}$ is *sit* provides the basis for predicting that the upcoming sounds will be /ɪ/ and /t/. This prediction could be realised by mirroring the neural activity associated with the articulatory process. At the level of grammatical act, *sit* may be interpreted as a verb and this will provide evidence for predicting what lexeme will be produced next. These hierarchical predictions cascade downwards, so the grammatical category helps predict what lexeme will appear next and what sounds will be heard. What this means is that, generally, higher-level representations facilitate the processing of linguistic sequences. In many ways this is what a language is. Furthermore, the fact that the utterance begins with a verb also provides evidence about the unrealised subject of the sentence (i.e., B) at the locutionary level. Finally, since B is the subject, the utterance has the force of a command, which takes us to the message A is communicating at the illocutionary level.

Now imagine that B predicted that A wanted to tell them to sit down. This prediction is based on mentalising. If B predicted that A wanted to tell them to sit down, then B would already be predicting the potential locutionary acts, the grammatical structure of the utterance, the words that are likely to appear and the sounds that are going to appear first. Making a prediction based on mentalising can be compared to predicting what the label on a door says based on a model of the corridor. However, this time the model is based on a model of the utterance producer. Equally, A will have an intention to tell B to sit down.

This intention can be used to predict the locutionary act, the grammatical act, the lexical acts and the phonetic acts that will be produced. Since these predictions are self-fulfilling prophecies, they trigger the production of phonetic acts, which in turn make predictions accurate.

Unless these predictions are wrong, A and B have no reason to be aware of them. This is the power of predictive processing models of utterance production and comprehension. There is well-established evidence from eye-tracking studies that comprehenders look at what someone is going to refer to before they actually do so (Altmann & Kamide, 1999; Sedivy et al., 1999). However, it is also worth pointing out that the description of comprehending *sit down* is a bit unusual. Most of our experiences of human utterances occur not as one-offs but in conversation that is made up of turns. Most of the time a turn directly follows another turn (which itself directly followed another turn). The turn-by-turn sequence of interaction provides a really good basis for predicting what the next utterance will be, so much so that producers often produce their turns in overlap with the end of another communicator's turn (see Levinson, 2012). One explanation is that people are so good at predicting what someone else is saying that they know when they are going to finish saying it.

Producers are also predicting how an interlocutor will react; if they do not react in an expected way, this will result in a prediction error regarding their own previous production. This occurs in an identical fashion to the corridor example established earlier. In this case, however, a prediction error of how B might react may have an effect on A's model of B or of their current activity, or their conversation, or their relationship, all of which form part of the context. A sufficiently specified context can determine the value of every variable relevant for predicting what utterance will be produced and what effect it will have. As discussed in Section 1.2.4, context includes the setting, the language to be used, a set of shared assumptions, the current activity and the producer's and comprehender's relationship. If these variables are well enough established, then a top-down prediction can be made without any requirement for people to be aware of mentalising or mirroring. In other words, in certain circumstances it is possible to predict everything based on context. However, it is typically the case that the number of variables involved in communication or the number of potential values each variable may take is large enough that total prediction is impossible.

Coupled with the model of pragmatic communication outlined so far, this theory provides an incredibly flexible notion of how producers and comprehenders manage to communicate. What I aim to do in the rest of this Element is show that it can accommodate gesture.

1.7 Summary

In this section I have outlined a model of communication using theories from Gricean pragmatics. I have argued that such a theory is consistent with what we currently know about the neural processes involved in intentional action and intention reading. I have shown how perception, action, utterance production and comprehension involve a hierarchical prediction.

In this summary I present the predictive hierarchy for communicative acts. In Figure 4, the arrows within the model are bidirectional to represent the notions of *upward completion* and *downward prediction*. A phonetic act causes something to be taken as a lexical act, but the prediction of a lexical act can be used to predict the phonetic acts that might occur. Figure 4 is also divided into production and comprehension processes. Starting with production processes, the top level is context. The next level is *what is meant / illocutionary act*. The illocutionary act is an act that satisfies the producer's informative intention. The next level down is *what is said / locutionary act*, which satisfies the communicative intention and therefore indirectly satisfies the informative intention. The next levels are the grammatical, lexical and phonetic acts. Each of these acts satisfies its respective intentions-in-action. The phonetic act represents the behaviour a producer actually produced and presumably is associated

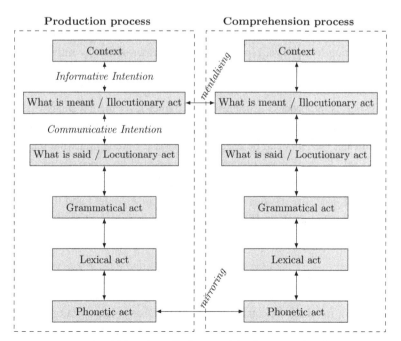

Figure 4 Multi-level predictive model of communicative acts

with the neurological representation of this motor act. The comprehender mirrors the production process using predictions based on three models. First, a model of context is used to predict the range of things a producer might do. Second, a model of the producer (via mentalising) is used to predict what a producer might intend to inform them of. And third, a model of the neural activity associated with the motor sequence involved in making certain noises is used to predict what phonetic act a producer is performing (via mirroring). The predictions in both production and comprehension processes are all occurring in parallel, so that predictions relating to what phonetic act is about to occur have an effect on predictions relating to what a producer means and vice versa.

In the next section I introduce gesture. I also outline how it has been treated in both the pragmatics and the gesture literature.

2 Incorporating Gesture into Pragmatic Theories of Communication

So far I have argued that we need to conceptualise communication as an inferential process where behaviours act as evidence for interpreting the reasons behind those behaviours. I have also argued that utterance production and comprehension involve cascading predictions over different levels of representation (pragmatic, semantic, grammatical, lexical, phonological). Two predictive processes facilitate inferential communication. The first, mirroring, is the process of representing lower-level representations of motor action by mirroring the neural activity responsible for that action. For example, interpreting speech involves the neural activity for forming certain speech sounds. The second, mentalising, is the process of representing higher-level mental states such as intentions. For example, if a comprehender knows what a producer intends to communicate, then this can be used as the basis for predicting what they are going to say. Both of these processes are supported by a rich set of shared assumptions (common ground) which include, but are not limited to, the language being used, the physical setting, the discourse context and the current joint activity. The question this Element aims to answer is what (if any) role gesture plays in this process.

2.1 What Is Gesture?

Example (1), in which M1 stated his preference for going upstairs when he gets onto a bus, was incomplete. Accompanying M1's speech was a complex gesture; this is represented in Figure 5.

tiśbūb	bark-īs	w-axayr	h-ūk	tiśbūb	aġawf
you.climb	into.it.f.	and-better	for-you.m.s	you.climb	up

'You climb into it and it's better for you to go up'

Figure 5 Example (1) with gesture

Here, M1's gesture depicts the paths he took stepping onto the bus and going up the stairs. This gesture, like all gestures, can be analysed as comprising multiple temporal phases: M1 goes from not gesturing to gesturing and then back to not gesturing. The temporal phases that constitute a gesture are often referred to as *preparation*, *stroke*, *retraction* (see Box 7) (Kendon, 2004). The stroke of the gesture is the most meaningful phase. An important question for analysing gesture is how a comprehender distinguishes between the preparation and the retraction phases and the stroke phase. One clue provided by producers is that it is almost always the case that the stroke of the gesture is temporally aligned with a semantically affiliated stretch of speech. Such alignment is so important to utterance producers that they often pause speaking or pause gesturing so that these two elements appear together.

Box 7 Phases of a Gesture Unit

Gestures are made up of three main phases:

- *Preparation phase*: Hands are moving from a resting position into the beginning of the meaningful part of the gesture.
- *Stroke phase*: The meaningful part of the gesture. It is the stroke that is representational.
- *Retraction phase*: Hands return to a resting position.

In the example, M1's gesture includes two strokes, each aligned with a clause headed by the verb *tiŝbōb* (lit. *go up*). It is important to point out how M1's language underdetermines the scene he is describing: *going up* into the bus and *going up* the stairs are two behaviours that may differ in a number of ways (such underdeterminacy is inherent in language (see Carston, 2002)). Thus, M1's gesture fills in some of the details underdetermined linguistically.

The first clause is accompanied by a gesture depicting the path M1 took to get onto the bus. Following this, M1 does not initiate a retraction phase but goes directly into another stroke phase, which accompanies the second clause. This stroke depicts the complex path M1 took to get onto the second floor. This path, while constantly moving upwards, first comes out to M1's right, then left, then vertically, before levelling off. In Figure 5 I have provided schematic representations of the paths depicted in these gestures. There are two observations to be made. First, notice that while the scene that M1 is describing included a path to the right, then left, from an observer's perspective, M1's gesture goes first to the left then the right. It is typical that producers produce gesture from their own perspective. Second, it might seem that the vertical upwards movement prior to levelling off is strange (there is no ladder at the top of the stairs to climb up). It is likely that the bus that M1 used has a 90-degree turn at the top of the stairs so that the user comes out of the stairwell in the central aisle, standing exactly one floor up from where they entered it but rotated 180 degrees. To achieve this in the gesture, M1 would have to produce an awkward movement, bending his hand back towards his face. Taking these two points together, just like the lexeme *tiŝbōb*, this gesture is underdeterminate. However, the point recognised by many working in gesture studies is that, when taken together, M1's language and gestural depiction are more determinate than either on their own. They are *co-expressive*.

Further, M1's gesture is an example of what is called a *representational* or *iconic* gesture. And while gestures may perform a range of roles during communication (Kendon, 2004), representational gestures are the focus of this Element. The reason for this is that such gestures are intimately tied to what a producer says. Typically, representational gestures depict action, motion or shape, or they may indicate a location or trajectory. They may be figurative or non-figurative (McNeill, 2015). Representational gestures often involve the hands depicting the spatial properties of some non-present object by drawing in abstract gesture space (McNeill, 1992, p. 89). Importantly, it is not simply the movements that have meaning; the space in front of the individual becomes a meaningful platform, an imaginary prop (Clark, 2016), without which the gesture would not mean anything.

The ways in which gesture and language represent things are quite different. The meaning of gesture is *global*, whereas the meaning of language is *compositional* (McNeill, 2015, p. 21). Global meaning relates to the fact that the meaning of the whole gesture determines the meanings of its parts. However, the meanings of the parts of a clause determine the meaning of the whole clause. The difference between global meaning and compositional meaning can be highlighted by thinking about utterance production from a temporal perspective. Recall that utterance production involves grammatical acts that are composed of multiple sequentially produced lexical acts that are composed of multiple sequentially produced phonetic acts. The temporal interval encompassing a phonetic act is embedded under a larger temporal interval encompassing a lexical act. And lexical acts are embedded under an interval encompassing a grammatical act. This fact essentially detaches the representation reflected in a grammatical act from time. In other words, the sequential ordering of lexical acts is determined by grammar. However, gestures have global meaning, which means that any temporal interval during the course of a gesture stroke will not contain a smaller gesture unit but will contain part of the stroke. This means that it is often the case that the temporal nature of gesture reflects the temporal nature of what is being represented. Gestures are a direct link between a speech event and a represented event.

Focussing only on illocutionary, locutionary and lexical acts, the difference between language and gesture is presented in Figure 6. This figure represents the temporal relationship between language and gesture using the concepts of sequential and simultaneous acts from Section 1.4. If the event *e1* refers to the speech event, then there are two simultaneous sub-events, *e1a* and *e1b*. The locutionary act occurs during *e1a* and the gesture occurs in *e1b*. As shown in Figure 6, the locutionary act comprises sequential lexical acts (*e1a.1–e1a.4*). The effect this difference has is that the movement in gesture which M1 produces is a temporal and spatial analogue (Clark, 2016) for the path he took on the bus, which is part of the represented event.

The concept of temporal and spatial analogue is fundamental for understanding what gesture means and provides the basis for Clark's (2016) theory of depiction, which includes representational gesture. Clark defines depictions

Illocutionary	{M1 told the researcher that he prefers to go upstairs $\}_{e1}$
Locutionary	{M1 said 'axayr hūk tiśbōb aġawf' $\}_{e1a}$
Lexical	{'axayr'$\}_{e1a.1}$ {'huk'$\}_{e1a.2}$ {'tiśbōb'$\}_{e1a.3}$ {'aġawf'$\}_{e1a.4}$
Gesture	{gesture stroke $\}_{e1b}$

Figure 6 Temporal relationship between language and time

as physical analogues of what they represent. Going back to M1, the path in his gesture was a physical analogue for the path he took on the bus. Clark's analogues involve three levels:

- the *distal scene*: the thing being depicted
- the *proximal scene*: the depiction itself
- the *base scene*: the physical characteristics of the depiction.

If we apply this to M1's gesture, we can state the following:

- Distal scene: M1 is depicting how he went up the stairs.
- Proximal scene: M1 is depicting an upwards trajectory (schematically represented in 5).
- Base scene: M1 is executing a behaviour involving his hands moving upwards.

Clark argues that the mapping from base scene to proximal scene is functional, but the mapping from proximal scene to distal scene is analogue. Because there is nothing inherent in M1's movement that means it should be interpreted as depicting how he climbed onto the bus, it is only with an *interpretive framework* that the mapping of proximal to distal can be made. The distinction between base, proximal and distal scenes is important because it provides further details on the relationship between the representational levels of language and gesture. The question, then, is how these different levels of gesture representation are related to the different levels of representation associated with communicative acts. However, before I address theories of gesture's role in communication, I want to explore what gestures are realisations of.

2.2 Idea Units

Traditionally, linguists interested in semantics and pragmatics discuss propositions. Propositions are defined according to whether they are true or false and as a result are regularly presented in a language-centric way. Utterances (in part) are realisations of propositions. Any propositional model of meaning that is attempting to model the relationship between thought and communicative behaviour is pushed to marginalise gesture owing to its non-propositional elements. One way to capture gesture's meaning is to assume that representations are modal. In other words, humans think about space spatially and think about language linguistically. In gesture scholarship, the concept of the *idea unit* has been developed to act as an underlying unit of thought which reflects both language and gesture (Kendon, 1980; McNeill, 1992, 2005).

Within pragmatics, Carston (2010, 2018) has developed a similar idea in relation to the imagery conveyed by metaphor. Carston (2018, p. 205) argues that memory images may be activated during linguistic interpretation. Carston's ideas build on the concept of *perceptual symbol systems* (Barsalou, 1983, 1999, 2008). Perceptual symbols are modal and analogical. A perceptual symbol is represented in the same systems as the perceptual states that produce them.

Although there is a large literature suggesting that imagery plays a vital part in language processing, Carston (2018, p. 210) does not recognise imagery as part of a producer's communicative intention in the context of metaphor. Images are treated as *epiphenomenon* or *incidental side-effects*. Carston (2018, p. 212) suggests that speakers and writers who are aware of the impact of such incidental imagery may be able to deliberately invoke it, but this does not mean that such imagery should be considered a fundamental part of a model of intentional/inferential communication.

Although Carston's theory is about metaphor, there seems to be a clear parallel between linguistic content + memory images and idea units. I believe that utterances comprising language and gesture are realisations of both imagistic and propositional representations. The question we need to answer is whether gesture is incidental, the product of images unintentionally evoked in the process of speaking, or whether gestures are produced to communicate their content.

2.3 Incorporating Gesture into Theories of Communication

In the next two sections I will introduce and explore the two main models of gesture production/comprehension discussed in the pragmatics literature. The first argues that gestures are not produced with the intention to communicate and the second suggests that gestures are communicative for the same reasons that linguistic acts are.

2.3.1 Gestures Are Shown, Natural Behaviours

The first view is that gestures are signs with natural meaning, but they can be deliberately *shown* (Grice, 1989) to an audience to communicate something more than their natural meaning. This view is most clearly outlined in Wharton (2009). In an earlier work, D. Wilson and Wharton (2006) draw on Hauser's (1996) distinction between *signs* and *signals* (discussed in Section 1.2.1).

In order to distinguish between signs and signals, Wilson and Wharton (2006) provide the example of shivering (which is a sign) and smiling (which is a signal). The direct function of shivering is to warm the body, whereas the direct function of smiling is to communicate affective states (Ekman, 1999). If shivering communicates that an individual is cold, then this is a derived function of shivering. An individual who is cold and shivering may deliberately stand in a way that allows someone to see how cold they are. Using Gricean terminology, they are *showing* evidence that they are cold. Going further, someone who is not cold may produce aspects of shivering (e.g., rubbing their arms and saying *brrrrr*). However, most people are not capable of fully producing a natural shiver. In a similar way, people automatically smile when they feel a certain way and this naturally communicates something about their affective state. Smiling is a signalling system that both producers and comprehenders have access to. Someone who involuntarily smiles might draw someone's attention to their smile, *showing* their smile. Equally, it is possible to recreate a smile without the associated affective state. The point of these examples is that if something inherently communicates something (i.e., communicates without an intention to communicate) then it can be *shown* and if it can be *shown* then it can sometimes be deliberately and approximately produced in order to communicate its natural meaning.

Wharton (2009) argues that representational gestures are shown natural signs (not signals) and this means that their direct function is to do something other than communicate. Wharton (2009, p. 149) focusses on the fact that producers 'are either unaware or, at best, only marginally aware' of the gestures they produce. Wharton (2009, pp. 151–2) goes on to argue, when discussing the work of McNeill, that 'the work of David McNeill is concerned almost entirely with "gestures" that are largely not under the communicator's conscious control … A better understanding of the role of gestures in non-verbal communication may be gained by making use of the idea that some "natural" gestures (in particular, "gesticulations") are deliberately shown, even if they have not been intentionally produced.'

If representational gesture is compared to shivering then it should perform a direct function other than communicating something to a comprehender. Shivering is a natural sign because it is a consequence of being cold. Wharton (2009, p. 153) argues that 'gesticulations are better treated as natural *signs* of the speaker's desire to help the speaker understand'. In other words, gestures are speaker directed, they facilitate the communicative process, information can be extracted from them and they can be deliberately shown in order to be part of the communicative process. If this is accurate then gesture can be quite easily inserted into a pragmatic model of communication because gestures are not the product of an informative or communicative intention. Gestures are epiphenomena which are produced during speaking. This mirrors Carston's (2018) view regarding mental images. If Wharton's theory is correct then it would be necessary to show that gestures are performing a speaker-directed function.

Type of sign	Relation of sign S to object O	Method of signalling
Icon	S resembles O perceptually	depicting a thing
Index	S is physically connected with O	indicating a thing
Symbol	S is associated with O by rule	describing as a type of thing

Figure 7 Clark's types of sign

2.3.2 Gestures Are Part of Composite Utterances

The alternative view argues that gestures are part of composite signals or composite utterances (Clark, 1996; Enfield, 2009, 2013; Kendon, 2004). Herbert Clark's (1996, p. 159) theory of signalling[12] uses Peirce's (1998) theory of signs as its foundation. Clark argues that there are three types of sign (see Figure 7). From these distinctions, Clark (1996, p. 160) posits a three-way distinction between methods of signalling (here I have used depiction instead of demonstration to reflect Clark, 2016).

The general idea is that these different methods of signalling underlie all communicative behaviours and are not necessarily acoustic or visual in nature. Further, Clark argues that every utterance is realised not in a single method of signalling but as a composite of multiple methods. Most signals (and aspects of signals) are composite in this way. Clark's point is that it is not necessarily the case that a producer decides to communicate via speech or gesture; rather, they choose a composite based on methods of signalling. In this respect, Clark's view removes the primacy of language from conceptualisations of communication.

According to Clark (1996), the choice of composite is determined by three factors: purpose, availability and effort. Purpose relates to the fact that certain purposes are only realisable (or most easily realised) by certain methods of signalling. If a producer's purpose was to draw someone's attention to an individual, it might be possible to do so by describing that individual, but it might be easier to direct a recipient's attention with eye gaze or a pointed finger. Equally, if a producer wanted to describe the spatial arrangement of furniture in a room, it might be easier to depict what it looks like with hand gestures or a sketch rather than to describe it. However, it is not always the case that all methods are always available. What if the producer is trying to describe the arrangement of furniture over the telephone or greet a neighbour when they have their hands full and their keys in their mouth? Effort relates to the fact that

---

[12] Clark's notion of signalling is distinct from the one discussed in Section 1.2.1. Clark's uses a more common sense notion that *signalling* refers to the use of a sign or signal.

different methods may be more efficient ways of signalling something. While Clark argues that there is no obvious metric for effort, this notion has been used to argue for avoiding redundancy across modalities (see McNeill, 2000). In summary, Clark's ideas of purpose, availability and effort can be used to model why someone produced a particular composite signal.

So, under the composite utterance approach to gesture, both language and gesture are communicative for the same reason. They are tools that provide evidence that guides the comprehender to the producer's informative intention.

2.3.3 Summary of Pragmatic Models of Gesture

The natural gesture and the composite utterance perspectives emerged out of the pragmatics literature. Both theories assume that gesture may be used by a comprehender to infer a producer's message. Where they differ is in their treatment of why gestures are produced. The natural gesture theory assumes that gestures are natural signs that may be shown. In the terminology adopted here, the composite utterance perspective assumes that gestures, like speech, are non-natural signs that are produced with the intention to communicate. However, these two theories both rest on assumptions that I believe to be flawed.

Assumption 1: Intentions require awareness. Wharton's (2009) argument for the natural gesture theory is that because people are not aware of their gestures, gesture is not intentionally communicative. The implicit assumption in Wharton's view is that for something to have non-natural meaning in the way Grice described, the producer must be aware of it. Bara (2010, p. 51) makes a similar claim: 'communication is openly intentional. That is, the actor wants her partner to recognize not only the informational content of the communication act but also that she is attempting to communicate something relevant. This implies that communicative activity is always conscious.'

The first part of this definition essentially repeats the definition of a communicative act in Box 4 from Section 1.2.6. However, Bara goes further and infers that this means that communicative acts are conscious. Bara reinforces Wharton's claim that gestures which are not under a communicator's conscious control are not the product of a communicative intention and should be considered to have natural meaning.

Kendon (2004) presents an argument that leads to the same conclusion from the point of view that gestures are communicative, but he disagrees with the whole notion of a communicative intention. Kendon (2004) argues that gestures have features of manifest deliberate expressiveness and that these features are perceived directly, requiring 'no deductive process leading to an *inference* of an intention' (Kendon, 2004, p. 15). Kendon (2004, p. 15) goes on to state:

Actions can be varied so that they have more properties that will lead them to be treated as intentionally expressive, or fewer of them. This fact in itself is evidence that the judgement of an action's intentionality is a matter of how it appears to others and not a matter of some mysterious process by which the intention or intentions themselves that may guide an action may be known.

These views all suggest that because people are not necessarily aware or conscious of their gestures, then gestures are not the product of Gricean communicative intentions. I believe that this view, whether or not it is made explicit, is problematic not just for understanding gesture but for understanding all communicative acts. Communicative intentions do not require us to be aware of every aspect of our communicative acts. In two papers, Campisi and Mazzone (2016; Mazzone & Campisi, 2013) have provided compelling arguments against the perspective that intentions require awareness. Their arguments rest on a similar idea to that proposed in Section 1.6. In the terminology of this Element, perception and action are based on cascading hierarchical predictions. If a prediction at a higher level is satisfied, then it is unlikely that someone will be aware of the predictions relevant to lower levels in the hierarchy. If an utterance producer intends to inform a comprehender of something, they are likely to predict how that comprehender will react. If a comprehender reacts as predicted, then there is no reason to consciously entertain what behaviour they produced. However, when producers are not successful in predicting how a comprehender will react, they become aware of their communicative behaviours. Producers may rephrase what they said, provide additional background information and, in many circumstances, produce gesture. While this is not an argument against the natural gesture theory, it is an argument against using awareness as a premise for such a theory.

Assumption 2: The efficient information fallacy (EIF). This assumption will crop up several times throughout the rest of this Element. It is essentially the same argument made in Section 1.6 regarding redundant information in speech. The story goes like this. Utterance producers are producing behaviours that communicate information. In speech, if the information presented is not all necessary, then the producer's utterance is not optimal. For example, if a producer referred to the only glass in a cupboard as *the tall glass*, then the word *tall* is unnecessary.

The notion of redundant information is regularly used in psycholinguistic experiments (see Degen et al., 2020, for a recent review). However, from a Gricean perspective, people regularly use informationally redundant information, not because they are not speaking efficiently but because they are communicating something other than what is typically encoded by language. While there might be some efficacy in using the notion of redundancy to describe speech, a problem arises when it is applied to utterances made of language and gesture.

Language and gesture are co-expressive. It is not the case that gesture supplements language; they both have a role in expressing an underlying meaning. While a gesture may communicate the same information as language, it is not redundant because they appear in different modes and these different modes relate to different modes inherent in an idea unit. McNeill (2012, p. 186) refers to theories of language and gesture that subscribe to a notion of redundancy as firehose theories because 'water pressure, crimped at one place (a breakdown in speech), causes a bulging out someplace else (a gesture)'. The firehose relates to the idea that gesture supports communicational difficulties in language (and perhaps vice versa). The inverse of this is that, all being normal, each modality should communicate unique information. If language communicates the same information as gesture, then one of them (it is almost always the gesture) is thought to be redundant. Alibali et al. (2009) developed a whole coding schema for language and gesture based around redundancy. In Clark's model, the composite signal notions of effort and purpose have been used as a basis for applications of the EIF (de Ruiter, Bangerter, & Dings, 2012).

The idea of redundancy seems to suggest that when gesture and language convey the same information, one is a waste of effort because both acts are realising the same purpose. The issue with the EIF is that it conceptualises communication as being about packaging a certain quantity of information rather than communicating a certain message, which may or may not be packaged into information in either speech or gesture.

Taken together, these two assumptions often lead to gesture being overlooked as a fundamental part of an individual's communicative practice. My point in this Element is that this misses the role of gesture in facilitating predications. Gestures are useful because they allow communicators to infer the reasons behind utterances. Their role is not always subject to awareness, but it is fundamental, as can be attested by people who are restrained from gesturing (Rauscher, Krauss, & Chen, 1996). I will return to this argument in Section 4.

In the rest of this section I outline the dominant models of gesture production within the gesture literature. Here, I will describe these models in terms of how they have emerged from Levelt's (1993) blueprint of the speaker. Such models represent utterance production as modular systems. At the end of this section I group the different theories, from both the pragmatics and the gesture literature, under what de Ruiter (2007) calls *architectures*, pointing out how they are linked.

2.4 Models of Gesture Production

According to Levelt (1993) (see Figure 8), the process of speaking begins with the conceptualizer. The conceptualizer is responsible for outputting a pre-verbal message to the formulator. The conceptualizer has access to the broader aspects of cognition, including a discourse model, situational knowledge and encyclopaedic information. In the next stage of Levelt's model, the formulator takes the pre-verbal output of the conceptualizer and outputs linguistic form which is encoded grammatically and phonologically. The output of the formulator is an internal representation of a token phonetic act (the phonetic plan). The formulator has access to the speech comprehension system so that an utterance is monitored at two points, during planning and once a phonetic act has been produced. This monitoring takes place in the conceptualizer and can feed into message generation.

Within Levelt's model, the pre-verbal message reflects the communicative intention. However, Levelt's model of communicative intention deviates from the standard Gricean one. For Levelt (and many psychological models that

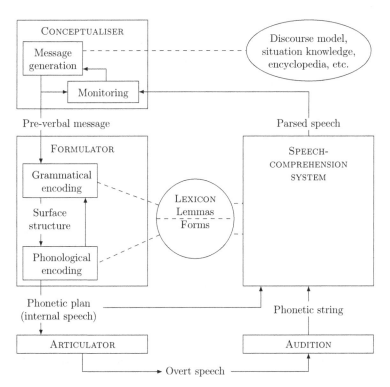

Figure 8 Model of speaking (based on Levelt, 1993)

have followed), *intentional* means consciously goal-directed and there is no requirement for the reflexive notion of communicative and informative intentions. According to Levelt's model, the *communicative intention* is based on the producer's desire to convey a certain piece of information linguistically (see Mazzone & Campisi, 2013). Therefore, Levelt's conceptualizer conflates the communicative, informative and social intentions of other theories. This model is capable of dealing with examples where the intention is to to assert something, but it does not go into detail regarding the relationship between an utterance and informative intention. This is another instance of the EIF. For example, if an utterance producer's informative intention was to inform their recipient that they were not up for going outside, how could this be linked with a pre-verbal message resulting in an utterance of *It's raining*?

In order to incorporate gesture into Levelt's model, we need to explore at which point in the process gesture is incorporated into utterance production. Three main models have attempted to do this.

2.4.1 Lexical Access Model

The lexical access model (Krauss, Chen, & Gottesmamn, 2000) (shown in Figure 9) is built on the idea that the direct function of gesture is not to communicate. In other words, meaning in gesture is not communicatively intended.

In the lexical access model, the pre-conceptualizer stage has been broken in two. First, long-term memory operates the same way as in Levelt's model. However, working memory is now included and subdivided into propositional and spatial/dynamic working memory. During speech production, lexical items are derived from *source concepts* in working memory. While source concepts may have spatial/dynamic features as well as propositional features, only propositional features are retained in the lexical representation. These are then processed in order to produce a phonetic output. The important thing to note is that the process of generating gestures is triggered by the auditory monitor. Gestures emerge as a response to a producer's own monitoring of their speech and, as such, do not have access to grammatical form or pre-verbal messages. In response to problems with lexical access during speech production, the auditory monitor triggers the motor planner to produce gestures, which are themselves derived from the spatial/dynamic features of the *source concept* that was activated during speech processing. Once the lexical item that is related to the gesture has been produced, this sends a message to stop the gesture. This model is called the *lexical* access model because when a producer is struggling to produce a particular lexical item, features of a gesture may help

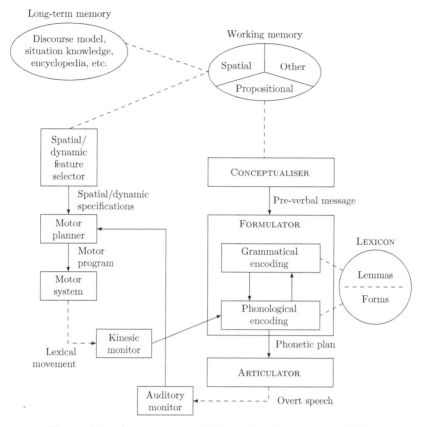

Figure 9 Lexican access model (based on Krauss et al., 2000)

facilitate production. So gestures are derived from spatial/dynamic representations in working memory, but they are not intentionally produced. Going back to the different levels of communicative acts represented in Figure 2, the lexical access model assumes that gestures are related to the lexical act, but that they are natural signs.

The lexical access model has a lot in common with the natural gesture theory. One major difference is that while Wharton does not specify how gesturing facilitates speaking, the lexical access model argues that it is centrally concerned with lexical access. Models such as the lexical access model and the natural gesture theory can be said to have a window architecture (de Ruiter, 2007) because gestures communicate by providing a window onto the producer's cognitive processes rather than being directly communicative. In other words, gestures are natural signs from which a communicative function can be derived.

2.4.2 Sketch Model and Tradeoff Hypothesis

The sketch model (de Ruiter, 2000) is shown in Figure 10. In this model, the
conceptualizer, which has access to both spatial and propositional working
memory, produces two outputs: a message and a sketch. The sketch becomes
the gesture component and the message becomes the speech component of an
utterance. The gesture planner signals to the message generator, which means
that message generation is partially determined by planned gesture. Here,
speech and gesture derive from the same communicative intention, but represent different features of it. This model has been developed into the tradeoff
hypothesis (De Ruiter et al., 2012), also called the mutual adaptive modalities

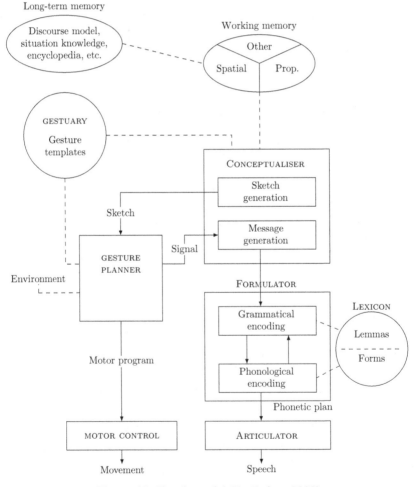

Figure 10 Sketch model (De Ruiter, 2000)

hypothesis (de Ruiter, 2006). The basic idea is that if the packaging of information in one communicative channel becomes more difficult then the other will compensate.

The trade-off hypothesis is based on Clark's notion of composite signal, and the sketch model can be thought of as a cognitive architecture capable of producing composite utterances. De Ruiter (2007) has referred to the sketch model as having a *postcard architecture* because, like a postcard, the sent message contains language and imagery, neither of which is subservient to the other. And, like a postcard, both elements are selected by the sender to be communicative. Information is packaged into both speech and gesture so that the composite output is informationally optimal.

2.4.3 Interface Hypothesis

The final model (Figure 11) is known as the interface hypothesis (Kita & Özyürek, 2003). The interface hypothesis assumes that gesture has its origin in action and is represented as spatial-motoric information in working memory. Further, the interface hypothesis stipulates that there is a bidirectional relationship between message and gesture generation. To represent this, Levelt's conceptualizer has been divided in two, a communication planner and the lower, subdivided action and message generators. The communication planner is responsible for communicative intentions and is responsible for roughly determining which information is to be represented in speech and gesture via the action the message generators, respectively. It is in the latter stage that the synchronisation of speech and gesture is determined. Another key feature is that the formulator feeds back into message generation, which in turn feeds into action generation. Therefore, this model assumes that gesture is generated in a parallel fashion with speech – they are inter-generated. The action generator is a general mechanism for planning action and as such can function somewhat autonomously. However, because feedback occurs only in the interaction between message generation and the formulator (and not between action generation and motor control), the process of packaging information for speech plays a more constraining role on the production of gesture than vice versa. One of the key differences between the interface hypothesis and the other two models is that the key process is the packaging of thought for language (or thinking for speaking, in the terms of Slobin, 1987). Therefore, whereas the lexical access model assumes that gesture is generated prior to speech and the sketch model assumes that gesture is generated autonomously from speech, the interface hypothesis assumes that gesture is fitted to linguistic structure.

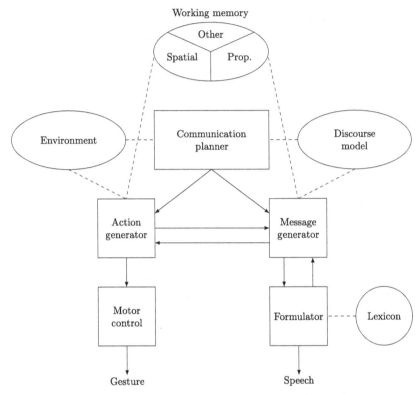

Figure 11 Interface hypothesis (based on Kita & Özyürek, 2003)

From the interface hypothesis, while both gesture and language are the product of a communicative intention, the production of language guides the production of gesture in a way that the production of gesture does not guide the production of language. De Ruiter (2007) has described the interface model as having a *language architecture* because the production of language constrains the production of gesture.

The interface hypothesis has similarities with both the natural gesture and the composite utterance theories. Like the natural gesture theory, the production of language constrains the production of gesture. And like the composite utterance theory, the direct function of gesture is to communicate.

2.5 Taking Stock of Gesture Production Models

The different perspectives of gesture production are summarised in Table 1. In this table I use the notions of type of sign, dominant mode and level to distinguish the different models.

Table 1 Summary of processing architectures

	ARCHITECTURE				
	Window		**Postcard**		**Language**
	Natural Gesture	Lexical Access	Comp. signal	Sketch Model	Interface Hypothesis
Sign	Natural	Natural	Non-Natural	Non-Natural	Non-Natural
Dominant mode	Language	Language	Neither	Neither	Language
Level	Locution	Lexical	Illocution	Illocution	Illocution

The lexical access and the natural gesture theories are grouped under the heading *window architecture*. Both theories assume that gesture is a natural sign because it does not have a direct function to communicate. They also assume that language dominates gesture. However, they make different assumptions about the representational level relevant to gesture production. For the lexical access model, gesture can be used to resolve issues in selecting a lexical item. For the natural gesture model, it is not clear how gesture helps speaking, but since it is not produced intentionally then it must be lower than the illocutionary level.

The remaining theories all assume that gesture is a non-natural sign since it is intentionally produced to communicate, but they disagree on the process. Under the heading *postcard architecture* are the sketch model and the composite utterance theory. Both assume that neither language nor gesture dominates and that gesture is the product of an intention to communicate, which means that communicating is its direct function.[13] Under the heading *language architecture*, the interface hypothesis assumes that language dominates gesture during utterance production. In terms of the different levels of communicative acts, these three models would all require gesture production to be engaged at the level of illocutionary act. However, since the models represent communicative intentions in a Leveltian way, it is not clear how they would cope with implied meaning. This is something I will pick up at the end of Section 3.

In order to disentangle these different models of gesture production, in the next section I will explore the experimental literature on gesture production.

---

[13] This is not intended to suggest that communication is gesture's only function or that gesture may not be presented in a way that is not obviously communicative (e.g., on the phone). The reason why humans gesture from an evolutionary perspective is to communicate.

Since the model of communication I am adopting here argues that comprehension and production are intimately linked, I will also explore the experimental literature on gesture comprehension.

3 Experimental Studies on Gesture Comprehension and Production

So far in this Element I have introduced a model of communication based on pragmatics and predictive processing. This model relies on the idea that during communication both producers and comprehenders make inferences using predictions based on higher-order regularities that make the process of production and comprehension more efficient. One of the core regularities used to make such predictions during communication is the idea that communicators intentionally produced behaviours from which the reason behind producing such a behaviour can be inferred. Mentalising is used to model a producer's intentional states and this process makes utterances easier to comprehend and produce. Mirroring is used to interpret phonetic acts by mirroring the neural activity associated with the motoric aspects of such acts.

Section 2 presented three processing architectures:

- A *window architecture*: gestures are not intentionally communicative but can provide the comprehender with a window onto the producer's cognitive process.
- A *postcard architecture*: gesture, like language, is produced to be communicative. Gesture and language adapt to each other in order to result in the most effective composite signal.
- A *language architecture*: gesture, like language, is produced to be communicative. Gesture is produced during the packaging of thinking for speaking and, as a result, gesture follows the structure of language.

In this section I investigate whether there is evidence to favour one architecture over the others. All the architectures assume that it is possible to process the information presented in gesture. The fact that we were able to extract information from M1's gesture in Figure 6 demonstrates that this is a fairly trivial point. There is also a wealth of evidence that people can extract information from gesture in real time (Beattie & Shovelton, 1999a, 1999b, 2001, 2002).

The three questions I aim to answer in this section are:

- What is the relationship between language and gesture?
- Why do people extract information from gestures?
- Why do people produce gestures?

3.1 What Is the Relationship between Language and Gesture?

In Section 2.2, I introduced the notion of an idea unit, which implies that, despite the fact that information is represented in different formats, there is an interaction between what might be called speech and gesture semantics. Is there evidence that such an interaction exists?

Evidence that there is a level of comprehension associated with an idea unit can be found in the fact that when someone receives information in both speech and gesture, they are often unable to recall the modality the information was presented in (Kelly et al., 1999). Furthermore, it appears that gestures are more strongly associated with related words than other words are (So et al., 2013). For example, a gesture depicting flying is more strongly associated with the word 'bird' than the word 'fly' is. This association appears to be mutual (i.e., it goes both ways) and obligatory (Kelly et al., 2015; Kelly, Özyürek, & Maris, 2010). Taken together, these observations are corroborated by neurological evidence where it has been shown that gesture and words that mismatch a syntactic context produce similar affects (Kelly, Kravitz, & Hopkins, 2004; Proverbio et al., 2015; Wu & Coulson, 2005, 2007). The association between language and gesture semantics is not simply functional; it appears to be associated with specific regions of the brain (Özyürek, 2014), suggesting that there is an amodal network for semantic processing. This network involves the left inferior frontal gyrus (lIFG), the medial temporal gyrus (MTG) and the superior temporal gyrus/sulcus (STS/S) (Özyürek, 2014; Straube et al., 2012; Willems, Öyürek, & Hagoort, 2007, 2009; Xu et al., 2009). These observations suggest that gesture and speech are tightly interconnected and processed together (Özyürek et al., 2007). There is further evidence that lower-level processing of speech sounds and visible gesture is done separately first before being integrated (Straube et al., 2012).

From the perspective of utterance production, it appears that speech and gesture are co-constructed semantically. Much of the evidence appears to show that while speech and gesture are related to the same idea unit, they may present information relating to different aspects of it (Beattie & Shovelton, 2006; Holler & Beattie, 2002, 2003). Furthermore, Cohen, Beattie and Shovelton (2011) showed that when speech and gesture are analysed at a semantic level, 81.8 per cent of gestures contained at least one semantic feature that was not present in speech. Finally, Melinger and Levelt (2004) demonstrated that people were more likely to omit information from speech that they produced in gesture. The conclusion to take from these studies is that in both the production and the comprehension of utterances, there is a strong suggestion that the information presented in speech and in gesture involves an amodal semantic network.

3.2 Why Do People Extract Information from Gestures?

In the discussion so far, the focus has been on the interrelation of meaning in speech and gesture. However, the comprehension of language involves interpreting behaviours (e.g., speech sounds) as embedded under hierarchically arranged levels of representation (e.g., phonetic < lexical). Following the processing architectures outlined earlier and since speech and gesture seem to be tightly interconnected semantically, it is worth exploring the way the different levels of gesture production mirror the differing levels of speech production. In H. H. Clark (2016; see also Section 2.1 of this Element), the physical act of gesturing is referred to as the *base scene* which is embedded under a *proximal scene* which is embedded under a *distal scene*. So in order to understand why people extract information from gesture, we first need to consider why people treat bodily movement (i.e., the base scene) as representative (i.e., the distal scene).

If we adopted assumptions of a language or window architecture, we could argue that the production of language alongside gesture is the primary reason people treat gesture as communicative. Indeed, the kind of gestures I am interested in here are often called co-speech gestures because they obligatorily appear alongside speech (McNeill, 2015), which makes it very difficult to remove speech as a deflationary reason for treating gestures as communicative. Novack, Wakefield and Goldin-Meadow (2016) demonstrate that while accompanying speech appears to be a reason why people treat manual movements as representational gestures, the more vividly a gesture depicts something the more likely someone is to treat it as representational regardless of it being accompanied by speech. Novack et al. (2016) also show that movements which serve no obvious instrumental purpose were treated as representational, which implies a predisposition for people to treat non-instrumental movements as communicative.

Eye gaze is another cue for interpreting someone's behaviour as communicative (Bara, 2017). The large sclera/white of the human eye relative to other primates has been hypothesised to be an evolved feature that aids communication (Kobayashi & Kohshima, 2001; Yorzinski & Miller, 2020). Not only does eye gaze inform comprehenders that they are being addressed but it has been demonstrated that speaking with averted eye gaze has a negative impact on language comprehension. However, when speech is accompanied by gesture, this negative impact disappears (Holler et al., 2014). The compensatory effect of gesture suggests that both eye gaze and gesture are important cues for interpreting speech and that, when necessary, gesture can compensate for a lack of eye gaze, which may be a critical aspect of interactions involving more than two people (Özyürek, 2002). However, the fact that gestures can compensate for a lack of eye gaze implies that eye gaze is not a necessary condition for interpreting gestures as communicative. Gesture must be communicative independent of eye gaze.

The evidence presented so far appears to suggest that there may be elements inherent to the base scene that result in a bodily movement being treated as representational. Trujillo et al. (2018) show that when people believe that someone is learning from their instrumental actions or representational gestures, they produce kinematically different movements from when they do not. Actions/gestures produced in a more communicative context are bigger and more complex. Trujillo et al. (2018) further show that comprehenders were able to tell whether the producer believed their actions/gestures were communicative. People were able to do this even when they did not have access to the eye gaze of the producers.

It seems that people pay attention to gesture because features inherent to the bodily production of gestures provide a cue that the movement is representational. This suggests that there is a correlation between the level of phonetic acts and the base scene. Furthermore, the evidence appears to show that it is not simply because a phonetic act is produced that a base scene is interpreted as part of a representational gesture. If representational gestures are representational in their own right, then mirroring could play an analogous role in speech and gesture comprehension, which might explain the compensatory affect of gesture when eye gaze is not available. However, the evidence so far does not explain whether mentalising plays a language-independent role in interpreting gesture. The question we need to ask is whether people treat gestures as representational because they treat them as intentional or, to ask it a different way, do people treat gestures as having non-natural meaning in a Gricean sense?

In Section 1.3, the different brain regions involved in the comprehension of action vs communicative action were discussed. It was suggested that an IPN is responsible for processing intentional communicative behaviours (Enrici et al., 2011). The IPN includes the brain regions associated with mentalising and mirroring. A key question is whether these regions are involved in the processing of communicative gesture.

Studies have demonstrated that the IPN is activated by communicative behaviour directed at an individual compared to that directed at someone else regardless of modality (Enrici et al., 2011; Redcay, Velnoskey, & Rowe, 2016). While not making reference to the IPN, Trujillo et al. (2019) explore the brain regions associated with determining whether a gesture is communicative. Trujillo et al. (2019) show not only that mentalising regions are activated when someone assesses the communicativeness of a gesture but also that there is a directionality in the activation of the mentalising and mirroring areas. When someone is asked to assess the communicativeness of a gesture, there is activation from the mentalising to the mirroring area. However, when someone is asked to assess a non-communicative aspect of a behaviour (e.g., the hand was used to perform the behaviour), the activation goes from mirroring to mentalising.

The studies outlined here suggest that there is close semantic association between language and gesture. They also suggest that there are features inherent to gesture that result in people treating them as representational. Finally, there is evidence that a reason people treat gestures as communicative is because they treat them as intentional in a manner similar to speech. All this points to the idea that, for a comprehender at least, gestures are communicative behaviours that are independent from but integrated with language.

3.3 Why Do People Produce Gestures?

So far it has been shown that language and gestures form an integrated semantic representation. It has also been shown that gestures are interpreted as communicative on the basis of their physical properties, regardless of the presence of co-occurring speech, and that they are interpreted as communicative because they are treated as intentional (i.e., the interpretation of gesture involves the mentalising regions of the brain). However, evidence that gestures communicate, even if they are treated as intentionally communicative, is not evidence that they are produced in order to communicate (Melinger & Levelt, 2004). A core question for pragmatic theory is whether gestures communicate because they are natural signs that can be shown (Wharton, 2009) or because they are non-natural signs, intentionally produced in order to communicate (Clark, 1996).

One potential argument against a fully communicative theory of gesture production is that gestures serve some purpose other than communicating. Such a purpose could be producer directed. This would be in line with the lexical access view, the natural meaning view, and therefore could be explained using a window architecture. From these perspectives, gesture is not produced to communicate; rather, it communicates because it provides a window onto the processes of speech production. There is a wealth of literature supporting the idea that gestures perform a producer-directed function.

For instance, gestures do facilitate lexical access (Krauss et al., 1995; Morsella & Krauss, 2004; Wesp et al., 2001) and speech fluency is improved when gesturing is permitted (Rauscher et al., 1996). However, it has been argued that lexical access cannot be the purpose of gesture (as the lexical access model assumes) because gesture rate has been shown to be affected by task complexity, but not by lexical complexity (Alibali, Kita, & Young, 2000). Further, cross-culturally gestural constructions have been consistently shown to reflect syntactic (rather than lexical) features of languages (Kita, 2009). In line with the notions of an amodal semantic network, these observations imply a view more closely associated with the notion that an idea unit is presented in speech and gesture.

Even if gesturing is not about lexical access, this does not mean that a window architecture cannot explain gesture since the natural gesture theory does not specify the level at which the producer-directed benefit occurs. From the perspective of natural gesture theory, the observation of any benefit to the producer acts as positive evidence. However, logically, gesture benefiting the producer does not provide negative evidence for the theories associated with either the postcard or the language architectures, which both assume that gestures are produced with an intention to communicate. The reason for this is that speaking to yourself may provide a benefit when compared to remaining silent, but that does not mean that an intention to communicate is not fundamental to understanding what someone means when they speak. Arguably, what would provide positive evidence for a language or postcard architecture and negative evidence for a window architecture is evidence that gestures are recipient designed. It is to this question that I now turn.

One of the most fruitful, but debated topics in gesture studies is whether mutual visibility has an effect on gesture production. It has been demonstrated that people still gesture when they are on the telephone (Bavelas et al., 2008) and that blind people gesture even when communicating with other blind people (Iverson & Goldin-Meadow, 2001; Iverson et al., 2000). These observations point to the suggestion that gestures are not communicative. However, it has been shown that while people do gesture when their audience cannot see them, the type of gesture is important. Representational gestures are affected by visibility (Bavelas & Healing, 2013). It is also the case that the physical configuration of interactants plays a role in the production of gesture. Gestures are produced to be maximally visible to all participants (Özyürek, 2002). And, as mentioned earlier, producers who know that a comprehender is going to learn from their utterances produce kinematically distinct gestures (Trujillo et al., 2018). Gestures produced to be communicative are larger, more visible and more complex. In other words, gestures appear to be designed to be maximally communicative within the physical context.

Common ground is a critical aspect of context for interlocutors. It has been shown that the more common ground people share, the smaller, the less precise and the shorter (in duration) gestures are (Gerwing & Bavelas, 2004; Holler

& Bavelas, 2017). This finding parallels the decreased precision in articulation over the course of an interaction (see Clark & Wilkes-Gibbs, 1986).

These findings suggest that when people want to make their gestures more communicative, they adapt them by making them bigger, longer and more complex. However, when the communicative content of gesture loses some of its importance (because it is already common ground), smaller, shorter and less-precise gestures are produced. Combined with the observation that people were more likely to omit information from speech that they produced in gesture (Melinger & Levelt, 2004), these findings are hard to reconcile within a model of gesture that assumes that gestures are fundamentally about making speech easier. This is because the needs of the addressee appear to be taken into account when producing gesture. Gesture, like speech, is recipient designed (Campisi & Özyürek, 2013).

I believe that these observations present insurmountable evidence against the natural gesture theory. Recall that the natural gesture theory assumes that the direct function of gesture is producer directed. One of the main arguments for this perspective is that producers are not aware of gesture in the same way they are aware of speech. In this situation, the natural gesture theory argues that gestures can be shown, but presumably only once a producer has become aware of the fact that they are gesturing. It seems difficult to reconcile this theory with the fact that producers design their gestures for their audience. It is for this reason that it makes sense to assume that gestures are an inherent part of a complex communicative process, the lower aspects of which (e.g., producing speech sounds) producers are not necessarily aware of. However, this lack of awareness is owing to the fact that we are aware of higher-level aspects.

From this argument, I believe that we can rule out the natural gesture theory and therefore the idea of a window architecture. If we rule out the window architecture, this still leaves open the debate between a postcard architecture and a language architecture. In order to distinguish between these two architectures, it is necessary to investigate how the information expressed through gesture relates to the information expressed through language.

3.4 Language or Postcard Architecture?

Before proceeding, it is necessary to reiterate two key points. First, it appears that language and gesture form idea units that are derived from an amodal semantic network. Second, certain information is more likely to be presented linguistically while other information is more likely to be presented gesturally. The question we need to address in order to explore the difference between a language and a postcard architecture is: if we assume the former point, what process governs the second? In other words, why is certain information presented in certain modalities? The language architecture assumes that the packaging of information for speaking plays a dominant role in the process. The postcard architecture assumes that there is some form of mutual negotiation between modalities. In this section I will explore the evidence for both of these viewpoints.

There is a large body of evidence suggesting that gesture parallels the syntactic structure of speech (Kita & Özyürek, 2003; Özyürek et al., 2005; Özyürek et al., 2007). For example, in languages where the manner and the path information of an event are produced separately as opposed to conflated (e.g., separate: *the ball went down the hill rolling* vs conflated: *the ball rolled down the hill*), people also produce separate gesture strokes for manner and path (Kita & Özyürek, 2003). This is also the case in English when path and manner are described separately (Kita et al., 2007). Furthermore, the effect of language on gesture structure disappears when participants are asked to gesture but not speak about scenes (Ozcaliskan et al., 2016). This suggests that gesture is constrained by the *production* of language and not by the language a person speaks. These findings appear to favour a language architecture.

Of the studies that directly explore the assumptions relating to a postcard architecture, the results have largely been negative. For example, So, Kita and Goldin-Meadow (2009) explore the language architecture by investigating narratives. They build on the observation that when people refer to the same person over the course of a narrative, they point to the same location in gesture space. In this way, the pointing gesture uniquely specifies a referent. In speech and writing, characters introduced earlier are often referred to using pronouns (e.g., 'he' and 'she'). Pronouns are generally vaguer than pointing since 'he' can refer to any male character and 'she' to any female. This means that the specificity of a pronoun is dependent on the gender and the number of characters in a narrative. According to the postcard architecture, which suggests that gesture will be used to compensate for the lack of specificity in speech, one might expect a narrative containing two male individuals to include more pointing gestures accompanying 'he' than one containing a male and a female character. However, So et al. (2009) found the opposite. Gestures were produced with more specific language, which is taken as evidence for a language architecture.

De Ruiter et al. (2012) attempted to test the tradeoff hypothesis, which is a key component of any postcard architecture. The tradeoff hypothesis states that when gesturing gets harder, producers will rely more on speech, and when speaking gets harder, people will rely more on gesture. De Ruiter et al. (2012) specifically attempted to test the second part of the hypothesis. Their study involved pairs of participants who could both see a collection of tangrams on a wall in front of them. One participant was presented with a tangram on a computer screen and they had to direct the other participant to that object so they could identify it. De Ruiter et al. (2012) manipulated two elements designed to affect the difficulty/ease of speech production. First, codability was manipulated by having tangrams of differing complexity. Second, common ground was manipulated by having participants direct their partners to the same tangrams. The general assumption for the tradeoff hypothesis was that harder-to-describe tangrams will result in more gestures and repeated tangrams will result in fewer gestures. They measured gesture using a rate of gesture per hundred words and found that gesture rate did not increase as difficulty increases, nor did repetition affect gesture rate. They argue that these findings are against the trade-off hypothesis.

The evidence presented so far appears to point to a model of gesture production in which context does have an effect on whether people communicate through gesture. It also appears that language has an asymmetric influence over the content presented in gesture. However, as shown by Cohen et al. (2011), 81.8 per cent of gestures contain semantic information not found in speech. Kita and Özyürek (2003) argue that this information comes *for free*. Even if this were the case, people are more likely to omit information in speech later in a conversation when it has already been communicated in gesture, which suggests that gestured information is taken to be added to common ground (Melinger & Levelt, 2004). Taken together, this provides strong evidence for a language architecture.

De Ruiter (2017) comes to the same conclusion, but uses these insights to develop a different model. De Ruiter's new model, *the asymmetric redundancy sketch model* (AR-sketch model), is identical to the sketch model except the sketch (which is now referred to as the imagistic part of the communicative intention) is dominated by message generation (which is now referred to as the propositional part of the communicative intention). The main claim of the model is that 'the information expressed in iconic gesture originates from the same communicative intention as the verbal part of an utterance does, and is shaped so as to be maximally redundant with that communicative intention' (p. 65). De Ruiter's (p. 62) argument for this model comes from the overwhelming evidence of the influence of speech on gesture and the fact that there is little evidence that the structure of gesture influences the structure of speech.

While de Ruiter accepts a language architecture (de Ruiter, 2017, p. 66), he argues that the interface hypothesis is wrong for two reasons. First, gestures in the interface model are not constrained in any way. Second, the two components of the interface hypothesis must have a way of matching language and gesture, which implies that that information can be translated, which would be cognitively taxing. In the rest of this section I will argue that the suggestion that gestures within the interface model are not constrained in any way is false. I will deal with the second argument in Section 4.

The sketch and the AR-sketch models both make the same claim that is made in Levelt's speaking model, namely, that the conceptualizer is responsible for the informative intention and the generation of a pre-verbal message. This essentially conflates the distinction between the informative and the communicative intentions. I make this claim on the assumption that within the modular architectures represented in Section 2.4, each module produces a single output. In the case of the speaking model and both the sketch and the AR-sketch models, the message generator is responsible for outputting the pre-verbal message. What is not clear is whether the pre-verbal message relates to what a producer means or whether it is a pre-verbal version of what is said. This may seem like a trivial issue, but it means that while message generation (the development of *what is meant*) has access to context, utterance generation (the development of *what is said*) does not.[14] It is placing too great a burden on a single module. The result is that the conceptualizer is responsible for generating *what is meant* and how this relates to *what is said*. This turns the process of communicating from one where evidence is presented and an intention inferred (i.e., a nonnatural sign) to one in which a signal is presented that may be translated into an intention. In other words, the intention involved in communication is about the packaging of information. When de Ruiter talks of a trade-off he is talking about which channel it is best to package information in. In doing so, de Ruiter is subscribing to the EIF.

This aspect of de Ruiter's perspective, I believe, is not present in the interface hypothesis. Recall that in the interface hypothesis the conceptualizer has been split in three: first, the communication planner and then at the next level down the two modules of action generator and message generator. What is critically different about this model when compared to Levelt's and de Ruiter's is that both the communication planner and the message generator (and the action generator, but indirectly) have access to the discourse model. Furthermore, the communication planner and the action generator (and the message generator, but indirectly) have access to the environment. It is possible to conflate *environment* and *discourse model* and call them *context*, incorporating both common ground and the physical setting. What this means is that context can play a

---

[14] This leads to a problem referred to as *Grice's circle* within the pragmatics literature. A solution to Grice's circle is that both what is meant and what is said are context dependent (Levinson, 2000).

separate role in the development of what is meant (via the communication planner) and what is said (via the message generator). It is for this reason that de Ruiter's claim that gesture is unconstrained is wrong. According to the interface hypothesis, gesture generation and message generation are highly constrained by context.

This leads me to my next point. The sketch model and the tradeoff hypothesis both seem to miss a key point about the composite signal model of utterance production. De Ruiter treats tradeoff as a condition of information packaging. However, tradeoff is not simply a condition of information packaging; it is a condition of what communicative tool can be presented. To return to an analogy from Section 1.2.3, this is akin to assuming that a carpenter's choice of what tool to use involves deciding which side of a hammer will work best. In communication, like carpentry, it is often most effective to use two tools at the same time. To capture this, it is of paramount importance that context impacts both the message a producer is trying to communicate (i.e., what is meant) and the choice of tool used to provide evidence so that a comprehender can infer that message (i.e., what is said/gestured). The interface hypothesis achieves this by allowing context to have an impact on the communication planner, the message generator and the action generator. Essentially, this means that it is possible to unite the interface and the tradeoff hypotheses if we assume that their key insights are operating at different levels. The tradeoff is one between the ease of incorporating context into the communication planner or the action/message generators, not between how to distribute information across speech and gesture. There is an interface in terms of what is being said, but a tradeoff when it comes to what is meant.

A representation of this model appears in Figure 12 (I have called environment the 'spatial model' so there is more similarity between the two aspects of context). This represents the processing architecture that I assume both producer and comprehender have access to.

I believe that the argument outlined here responds to De Ruiter et al.'s (2012) first argument that gesture is not constrained in any way. Both language and gesture are constrained by context. However, de Ruiter's second argument relates to the problem of how information presented in gesture is related to information in language. De Ruiter's redundancy is one way to deal with this problem. Kita and Özyürek (2003) argue that it is the packaging of information for speaking that constrains gesture. However, de Ruiter argues that this implies that there needs to be a process of translation between information to be presented in gesture and that to be presented in language. In the final section of this Element I will provide an explanation of this process using the predictive model developed in Section 1.6.

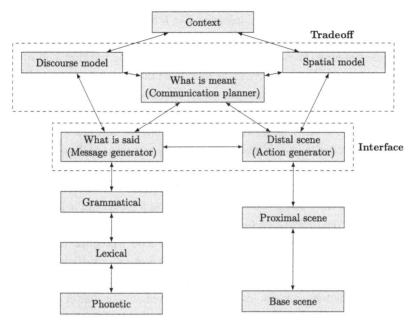

Figure 12 Interface and tradeoff in one model

4 Prediction, Communication and Gesture

4.1 Taking Stock

To summarise the view so far, human communication should not be thought of as being exhausted by the production and comprehension of signals, but as fundamentally involving the production and comprehension of non-natural signs. These non-natural signs provide evidence from which a comprehender can infer the reason the sign was produced based on the assumption that the producer intentionally produced it for that purpose. In order for all of this to work, such inferences, including the inference that resulted in the utterance producer producing the non-natural sign they did, involve prediction over multiple levels. From the bottom up,[15] communicators are predicting the phonetic acts to be produced. This prediction is partly made on the basis of the lexical acts those phonetic acts could be part of. Communicators are also predicting the lexical acts that will be produced next. This prediction is partly determined by the grammatical act it is assumed that each lexical act is part of. Communicators are also predicting how those grammatical acts relate to the world, in the form of locutionary acts. Locutionary acts relate to the question of *What did a*

---

[15] I am not suggesting that predictions are bottom up; this is just the way I am presenting the hierarchy.

producer say? And may include questions like *Who is being referred to?* This is partly determined by assumptions relating to common ground (e.g., '*Who do we know that might be referred to?*') and the idea that the producer said what they said for a particular reason, in the form of an illocutionary act. One of the most critical aspects of common ground for human communicators is the fact that we share a conventional linguistic system. This pairs the reason for saying things with the things said. However, it is not simply the case that what is said is always paired with what is meant. Illocutionary acts relate to the question of *What did a speaker mean? Why did they produce that locutionary act?* One of the reasons human communicators are able to work out what a producer means based on what they said is that we are able to use a model of the producer's mind to work out their reason for saying what they did. At this level, comprehenders use predictions based on what we assume about a producer to work out what they mean. Now, because this model is hierarchical, a sufficiently good prediction at the level of common ground and mind reading can lead to more accurate predictions at every lower level. If I predict your reason for saying something then I can predict what you are going to say, what its grammatical structure will be like, what lexical items it will contain and what sounds I am about to hear. At the bottom stage, the stage of motoric action, comprehenders mirror the neural activity associated with what they think a producer is going to say. If this prediction is accurate, then they will hear what they are expecting to hear and see what they are expecting to see. Finally, producers are also using predictions based on comprehension processes to guide their acts. They predict how a comprehender will react, but they also predict the sounds they will hear coming out of their own bodies.

In the last two sections I have explored how gesture might be incorporated into this picture. What we have seen is that gesture facilitates the comprehension and production of utterances. However, the meaningful content of gesture, which may enhance the meaningful content of speech, typically follows the grammatical structure of an utterance. This has been used to argue for a language architecture, where gesture is constrained by language. In this last section I provide an explanation of this process using ideas from pragmatics.

4.2 Turbo Codes

Most cognitive models of pragmatics start by dismissing the *code model* of communication. I did this in Section 1.2.2 when I argued that utterances are not signals. According to a code model, a transmitter at one end converts a message into a code that is decipherable at the other end by a receiver. The reason why this model fails to capture human communication is because conversion is about the quantity of information in the message and not the quality of information (Bara, 2010, p. 9). Essentially, the code model asks only what was said and not why it was said. Bearing this in mind, it might seem odd that I am about to begin this section by returning to the notion of encoding in order to propose a solution to the theoretical difficulties that present themselves when integrating gesture and pragmatics.

Rather than focussing on the whole communicative process, as is done with the code model, I simply want to focus on the role of error correction used by modern-day transmitters and receivers when encoding and decoding information. I am using Pearl and Mackenzie's (2018) description of the process as a starting point. When I speak on my phone, my voice is digitized. That is, my voice is converted into a binary code of 1s and 0s. These 1s and 0s are converted back into spoken language by the receiver. Each 1 and 0 is commonly referred to as a bit of information. So far, so code model. However, where the story gets interesting is that no transmitter or receiver is perfect so, in the process of transmitting and receiving, some 1s randomly become 0s and some 0s randomly become 1s. In order to correct for errors, it is possible to apply a fairly simple process of encoding each bit three times and decoding these strings of three bits as the average bit represented. So, if *1* is encoded correctly it will be represented as *111*, which by average will be decoded as *1*. Similarly, if there is an error and *1* is encoded incorrectly as *101* then it will still be decoded as *1*. If we assume that there is a degree of error in the encoding and decoding, then the more times a bit is encoded, the less impact the error will have. This form of error correction reduces error by introducing redundancy. However, reducing error is incredibly resource-intensive because it requires every bit to be encoded multiple times.

Claude Berrou solved this problem when he introduced *turbo code*. Rather than encode bits into a single codeword by re-duplicating them, he encoded bits into two codewords, once directly and once scrambled. From these two codewords, the original message can be decoded with 99.99 per cent accuracy. The exact mechanism of how this works is complex, but the point of this example is summarised by Pearl and Mackenzie (2018, p. 126), who state: 'To put it simply, two copies of code *A* are better than one.'

There is a parallel here between telecommunications and utterance production/comprehension. What makes a turbo code more accurate is not just that it is repeated but that the information is presented in a scrambled format. One possibility is that gesture increases the accuracy of prediction by reducing the amount of error associated with what someone wants to communicate based on what they did. How could gesture do this? Because gestures present information in a different format from language. As I argued in Section 2, the meaning of gesture is global whereas the meaning of language is compositional. Language and gesture are two tools that represent meaning in two formats but that are employed to achieve the same goal.[16]

Within biology, *degeneracy* is used to describe systems where two separate structures achieve the same function (Mason et al., 2015). Winter (2014, p. 961) posits that in a system which is characterised by degeneracy, 'components fulfilling the same function are different from each other, and they may simultaneously perform additional functions in other domains'. This should be contrasted with redundancy, where 'structurally equivalent or repeated system components realize the same function' (Winter, 2014, p. 961). It seems that error correction by repeatedly encoding the same bit employs redundancy, but turbo codes use degeneracy.

Winter (2014) argues that degeneracy is characteristic of spoken language, which makes transmission through language robust. One example Winter presents is voicing, which distinguishes certain words (e.g., **p**in and **b**in). One of the main cues that characterise the difference between a voiceless /p/ and a voiced /b/ is voice onset time, which refers to the length of time between the end of the sound and the onset of vocal fold vibrations. Winter points out that several other cues also distinguish voiced from voiceless sounds such as the pitch in the following vowel, the duration of the preceding vowel, the duration of the consonantal closure, as well as loudness differences within the voice onset time. All of these cues can be thought of as separate components all serving the same function. I believe that taken together, language and gesture are degenerate in this way, and as a result help ensure that communication is robust.

Within the predictive model of communication I have been developing in this Element, this means that a prediction made regarding what a producer meant based on both speech and gesture is more robust than one that includes only speech or gesture. As I argued in Section 1.6, predictive models of cognition suggest that reducing prediction error results in more-efficient perceptual processes. It follows that reducing prediction error in communication will result in more accurate communication. If this is right, then rather than being incidental, gesture is fundamental to communication not just because it has the potential

---

[16] One reviewer pointed out a problem with this analogy. For turbo codes, the same information is presented twice with one presentation being scrambled. In a sense, both encodings present the same information in its entirety and in the same format (some sort of binary encoding). However, when we communicate using language and gesture, different information is often presented in the two modalities. Part of the reason for this is that language and gestures employ different formats. However, language and gestures are still only communicating a single underlying message, not two messages that coincide. What I am focussing on in the analogy is not the way the information is coded but the fact that one message that is double-encoded is more predictable.

to communicate unique information but because it increases the likelihood of accurate prediction.

I suggested in Section 2.3.3 that two assumptions within the pragmatics literature have made the integration of gesture difficult. The first is that intentions require awareness. The second assumption is that information should be encoded in a non-redundant way. I referred to this second assumption as the EIF.

A predictive model of utterance production addresses both of these assumptions at once. First, if we adopt a predictive model, then lower-level processes (e.g., sound production, manual movement) do not have to be brought to the level of conscious awareness if they are determined by predictable higher-level processes. That is, if a producer predicts the impact of a particular communicative behaviour comprising both speech and gesture, there is no need to consciously predict the impact of either alone. Furthermore, if a comprehender predicts what a speaker is going to mean, there is no reason for them to be aware of how this meaning arose. What's more, since locutionary acts involve language and language is the conventional pairing of behaviour and representations, it is easier to bring to mind what someone said. Gestures, however, are not conventional in this way. This results in it being harder to detach gesture from the speech event, which has the effect that we are less aware of gesture. However, this does not mean that we are able to predict everything. Communication is complex and we make prediction errors all the time. These errors may bring to consciousness things that we are not normally aware of. Part of the role of gesture is that a prediction error related to language may be overcome by an accurate prediction of a gesture. Just like reading someone's lips can facilitate our understand of the words they are saying.

The EIF assumes that producers make decisions about efficiency over the information contained in an utterance. If information is re-duplicated, then it is not efficient. This idea is present in many Gricean theories of reference and encapsulated in de Ruiter's notion of trade-off. Thinking just in terms of language first, the general idea is that a producer chooses what to say from a range of possible locutionary acts that would communicate the same content. The locutionary act they actually chose is the one that communicates the message most effectively while costing the least. This act could be called the optimal locutionary act. Any information that is contained in an utterance that is not part of the optimal locutionary act is seen as being redundant. The problem with this perspective is that utterance producers regularly behave in a non-optimal way. The same idea is often applied to gesture. Imagine that a certain locutionary act is optimal, but that act is paired with a gesture that communicates the same information. This gesture is redundant since both speech and gesture communicate the same information. If we assume that utterance produbers are behaving optimally, then the information in gesture should complement the information in speech. However, as the studies in Section 3 show, people produce redundant information across speech and gesture. Regardless of this evidence that producers do not produce optimal utterances, the EIF is still alive and well in thinking about utterances.

One reason why the EIF prevails is that scholars treat communication as a form of signalling rather than an exchange of non-natural signs. To show why this is wrong, consider another analogy. Imagine that I want to place a bet on who will win the next World Cup. In a perfect world, I would put all of my money on the team I think will win, since if I am correct this will result in the biggest payout. In order to influence my decision, I may draw on knowledge relating to the teams, perhaps expert knowledge from others. If I was a particularly nefarious character, I could bribe or poison the players of the other teams. The main thing is that my goal is to win big by whatever means necessary.

When we apply this analogy to communication, there is one big flaw. In the betting example, I want to win. However, communication is not about winning. It is about placing an accurate bet. I produce the behaviour that has the best chance of communicating my message and not the most efficient way of communicating it.[17] Going back to the betting example, this would be like having a goal of betting on the winning team and not making the most money. If betting on the winning team is our goal then one strategy is to bet on every team. It is not quite that simple, though, since the better might not have an endless supply of cash, so they eliminate the teams that are least likely to win, leaving a selection of teams that they can bet on amongst which the winner is very likely to be. Going back to language, this process of eliminating utterances that are not likely to be useful, while keeping the ones most likely to communicate a message, will almost certainly result in redundant utterances, but this seems to be a better representation of the utterances that people produce. They are acts that are the most likely to allow a comprehender to draw the correct conclusion once the least likely ones have been removed.

In summary, it is entirely possible for an utterance to be informationally redundant (at the level of what is said) but not inferentially redundant (at the level of what is meant). When we think about the relationship between language, gesture and what a producer means$_{NN}$ to communicate, it makes more

---

[17] A potential objection to this analogy is that it frames communication from the perspective of the individual. However, my point is that good predictions are good for all parties and it is important to stress that both utterance producers and utterance comprehenders are making predictions simultaneously. It is as though both/all parties are betting on each other, accurate bets accumulate and everyone takes a share in the winnings.

sense to talk about degeneracy than redundancy. Discussion of information redundancy between language and gesture is not likely to be fruitful for pragmatic theories. Speech and gesture composites are better thought of as 'turbo utterances' where the same message is communicated by representing that message in two degenerate codes: one language, one gesture. And the recipient of such a message has a better chance of inferring what a producer wanted to communicate than if the message was conveyed only once. The reason why I think this is a novel approach to utterance production and comprehension is because it takes seriously the theoretical underpinnings of two fields: pragmatics and gesture studies. As a result, it upholds some basic ideas:

- Neither language nor gesture is primary; both have the potential to communicate.
- Utterances are not just carriers of meaning; they are pieces of evidence used to work out why the utterance was produced.
- As pieces of evidence, language and gesture co-strengthen each other in a degenerate way.
- The extent to which an utterance producer can predict how their utterance will be interpreted is an important factor in determining the composition of that utterance.

It is this last point that I believe will take the most work to explain. In the rest of this Element I want to make the claim that gestures are produced because they make it easier to predict how an utterance will be interpreted and they do this because gesture and language interact with different representational resources.

4.3 The Interface Model as a Predictive Model

The question that needs to be answered in this section is how does gesture aid the predictive processes of producing and comprehending communicative acts? I will use the interface hypothesis (Kita & Özyürek, 2003) to provide an explanation. Recall Figure 12, which presented a model combining the insights of the interface and the tradeoff hypotheses. It is possible to interpret this model as a predictive model of multimodal utterance production and comprehension along the following lines. The highest-level representation is context. Context is a model of the set of assumptions that two people are believed to hold (their common ground). In the interface hypothesis there are two models that play a role in determining utterances: the discourse model and the environment. Here, I have replaced environment with a spatial model. I am assuming that a discourse model is a set of assumptions that include the language being used, the previous utterance, the relationship between the interlocutors and their roles in the current exchange. A spatial model includes a set of assumptions about the spatial setting (what might be called their visual common ground (Rubio-Fernández, 2019)) but also about the general distal scene being described. For example, if someone was talking about getting on a bus, then a spatial model would include a spatial representation of a bus. The idea is that a sufficiently specified discourse and spatial model can be used to predict everything below. There are two necessary points to make. The first is that both the discourse model and the spatial model are used to predict *what is meant*, but this does not mean that their roles are equal. For example, a scripted ritual such as a marriage ceremony is one where the discourse model can be used to predict exactly what will be said next. Equally, in a situation where two people are communicating under water, the spatial model will be of greater importance for predicting someone's behaviour. The second point is that while the union of the discourse model and the spatial model could theoretically be used to make perfect predictions, it is unlikely that this would ever work in practice.

The next level in the hierarchy is labelled *what is meant*. What is meant is a model of the reason (informative intention) why an utterance was produced and (via the communication planner) used to predict how the informative intention will be satisfied by both speech and gesture. In other words, it is a model of the producer's intention. What is meant is a higher level of representation than either *what is said* and the *distal scene*. In other words, a sufficiently specified model of *what is meant* can be used to predict both *what is said* and the *distal scene*. *What is said* and the *distal scene* are both semantic representations and, as a result, can be used to laterally predict each other. However, *what is meant* is not the only model that can be used to predict *what is said* or the *distal scene*. *What is said* is directly predicted by the *discourse model* and the *proximal scene* is directly predicted by the *spatial model*. What this means is that it is entirely possible to predict what someone will say without having a decent model of their intention, so long as the discourse model can be used to predict their utterance. For example, imagine approaching a counter in a shop. We can be fairly certain what the person behind the counter will say despite the fact that we know nothing about what they are thinking when we approach them.

The lateral prediction between *what is said* and *proximal scene* is one of the key insights of the interface hypothesis. It has been used to suggest that gesture is redundantly fitted to language, but I think that this is a mischaracterisation. Instead, what it means is that a *discourse model* can indirectly predict gesture. Language, because it includes the conventional pairing of representations and acts, is highly predictable. So it is likely that in most cases a *discourse model* is a better basis for predicting what someone will communicate than a *spatial model*. This gives the impression that gesture is redundant, but what is really happening is top-down prediction based on the *discourse model*, which does a better job of predicting what someone will say.

The tradeoff in when to use language and when to use gesture is not about the information contained in either language or gesture; the trade-off is based on how easily *what is meant*, *what is said* and the *distal scene* can be predicted on the basis of a *discourse model* or a *spatial model*. When we think of it this way, we should expect redundancy because language and gesture together are more predictable than either alone. However, we should also expect that in situations where a *discourse model* is a poor predictor of *what is meant* and/or *what is said*, we should find people gesturing more. I will refer to this idea as the *predictability hypothesis*.

It is necessary to distinguish evidence for the predictability hypothesis from evidence that people are producing gestures to communicate. It might be argued that the predictability hypothesis explains the fact that people produce gesture even when gesture is not obviously communicative (e.g., on the phone). If we assume that the natural home of communication is a face-to-face setting, then communicative strategies that typically work in a face-to-face setting are likely to be the ones people adopt. If someone adopts a communicative strategy for face-to-face settings that includes a high rate of gesture, then this is likely to be transferred into other situations regardless of the communicative status of any gesture. Some evidence for this view can be found in the fact that prohibiting gesture increases speech disfluency (Rauscher et al., 1996).

Generally what we need is evidence that in situations where gesturing increases predictability, it is more likely to occur. I do not believe that anyone has tested this question directly, but studies have found evidence that appears to endorse it. For example, it has been shown that increasing complexity of tasks, which is likely to reduce the predictability of the confidence someone has in their utterances, increases gesture rates (Alibali et al., 2000; Hostetter & Alibali, 2007; Hostetter, Alibali, & Kita, 2007; Kita & Davies, 2009). Being permitted to gesture also has a positive impact on remembering word lists and spatial arrays (Goldin-Meadow, 2001). Interestingly, people who do not normally produce gesture do perform similarly in memory tasks regardless of whether they were permitted to gesture (Wagner, Nusbaum, & Goldin-Meadow, 2004). These findings could be interpreted as being related to the role of gesture in increasing the predictability of future utterances. Furthermore, it is not just that gesturing conveys a functional benefit; rather, the production of gesture is related to lower levels of spatial and visual working memory capacity, spatial transformation ability and conceptualisation ability (Chu et al., 2014). It has also been demonstrated that people with high visualisation skills and low verbal skills (phonemic, not semantic) gesture more (Hostetter & Alibali, 2007).

Taken together, this evidence points to the idea that gesturing can offload some of the cognitive burden associated with spatial working memory, but it can also compensate for lower verbal skills. All of this is in line with the ideas of the predictability hypothesis. The general idea is that when using a spatial model to predict utterance meaning is easier and/or when a discourse model is worse, then people will gesture more. The predictability hypothesis also suggests that people for whom gesture is a more reliable predictor of communicating something will produce more gesture. It is important to point out that this does not suggest that there will be a negative impact on the rate of speech with an increase in gesture, nor that there will be a reduction of gesture with an increase in speech. Predictability does not necessarily imply that something will not be said.

A question we need to ask, then, is how does prediction of speech and gesture relate to the broader question of inferring what someone meant based on what they said? Recall that predictions about what is meant are the result of mentalising and that predictions about the behaviour executed (i.e., phonetic act and physical act) are the product of mirroring. Of course, these two types of prediction should interact. If it is possible to mirror the behaviour an individual will execute, then it is possible to predict what a person will say and if it is possible to metarepresent their intention (i.e., what is meant) then it is possible to predict the various things they might say that would satisfy that intention. In other words, *what is said* sits in between predictions based on mentalising and predictions based on mirroring. I believe that predictions regarding *what is said* are drawn from three sources: mirroring the neural activity associated with executable behaviours, mentalising intentions, and a model of context.

The problem a comprehender faces when mirroring the neural activity associated with a phonetic act is that the act is not directly mapped onto what is being described. To give a concrete example of what I mean, take the following:

(18)   A man walked onto the stage.

(19)   There is a stage; a man walks onto it.

Example (18) presents a standard simple English sentence which describes a distal scene. In it *a man* appears first because it is the subject of the sentence. *The stage* appears later in the sentence because it is not the subject. However, if we imagine the distal scene described in (18) or we were to witness it, the stage would have to appear before the man could walk onto it. A more complex sentence is presented in (19); it reflects the temporal nature of the distal scene. What this means is that temporal prediction cannot play a direct role in working out what lexical act will be done next. It is for this reason that the discourse model, which includes the language being used, is used to predict what will be said because the temporal nature of the speech event is not particularly useful. This reduces the efficacy of mirroring for interpreting *what is said* and results in people relying on a discourse model and mentalising.

But what about gesture? I believe that gestures are easier to mirror because they involve base scenes that can be functionally mapped onto proximal scenes which are analogues for distal scenes (Clark, 2016). What we predict when it comes to mirroring gesture is not what is represented in the stroke (i.e., the distal scene) but what Heyes (2018) calls a *perceptual sequence*. Heyes argues that perceptual sequence learning is key to understanding imitation. Humans learn to pair a perceptual sequence, such as the sequence of movements involved in raising an arm, with a motor sequence (i.e., the sequence of action components involved in raising your own arm). Once these sequences are paired (in matching vertical associations) then it is possible to predict a perceptual sequence based on a motor sequence. In other words, it is possible to predict observed action by mirroring the neural activity associated with it. Taking this idea, we can argue that gesture is a perceptual/motor sequence involving (at least) three phases (outlined in Section 2): preparation, stroke and retraction. What I am arguing is that during interaction, comprehenders predict these three phases by mirroring them. In other words, a preparation phase gives rise to a prediction that a stroke phase will follow. It should come as no surprise, therefore, that when people try to make their actions/gestures more meaningful, they increase the complexity or size of the gesture stroke.

Furthermore, since gesture strokes are almost always coupled with semantically affiliated speech, then this pairing may also be predicted. The point is that people are likely to predict upon seeing someone raise their arms (preparation phase) that the gesture stroke will occur in the presence of speech and such a prediction may facilitate higher-level processes such as representations of *what is said* and *what is meant*. As a result, the predictions made about gesture may improve the accuracy of predictions made about communicative content in the absence of other visual cues such as mouth patterns. When speech and gesture are produced together, there is a lateral prediction from distal scene to what is said and from what is said through the hierarchy down to phonetic act. This explains the finding that gestures make it easier to process language when a producer is not looking at a comprehender. Finally, because I assume that the process of message generation has only indirect access to a spatial model, using gesture can facilitate predictions in this way as well. In other words, it facilitates the use of spatial deixis. In the next section I will present examples that provide evidence for the predictability hypothesis.

4.4 Some Illuminating Examples

In the last section I presented a model of utterance production and comprehension based on the notion of predictability. It is possible to explore the functionality of this position using two examples. I believe that these examples present problems for a language architecture because in both examples language causes problems that are solved by gesture. The examples are taken from J. Wilson (2016). The data comprises a small corpus of eight dialogues recorded during a lab-based task where one participant (the information giver or G) is required to describe a route on a two-dimensional map so that the other participant (the information follower or F) can draw it on their map. Crucially, the two participants cannot see each other's maps.

4.4.1 Second-Person Gestures

Most gestures are produced from the producer's perspective and the comprehender is required to invert any reference to horizontal left/right axis. In other words, a producer uses a spatial model that represents left/right from their perspective and this is mapped via distal scene and proximal scene onto the base scene of their gesture.

So, for example, if a producer describes a scene from a video (distal scene) in which a character moves from the left to the right of the screen and produces a gesture (base scene) of this movement, their gesture will also depict the movement from the producer's perspective. However, this means for the comprehender that the base scene is a left/right inversion of the distal scene.

Occasionally, people will produce a gesture from a comprehender's perspective in order to make the communicated content more transparent (this is typical of instructors giving gym classes). The downside (for the producer) is that they are required to invert their own representation of an event before they produce an utterance. If we imagine an utterance that includes direct reference to *left* or *right*, this means that a producer is having to simultaneously represent two spatial frames, where the word *left* is accompanied by a gesture using their right hand. This would make predicting the base scene of gesture much harder because it is not predicted by either language or the distal scene. This leads to an additional cognitive burden. The expectation, therefore, is that this additional cognitive burden will make it more difficult for a producer to predict the communicative impact of their utterance.

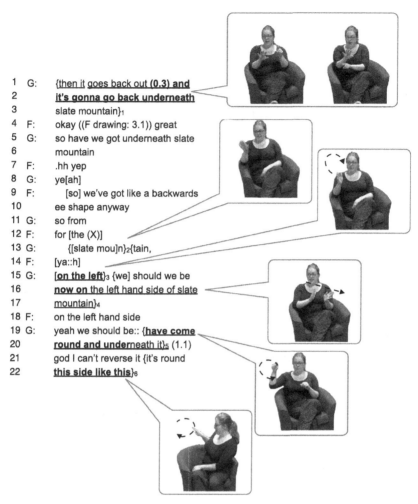

```
1  G:   {then it goes back out (0.3) and
2        it's gonna go back underneath
3        slate mountain}₁
4  F:   okay ((F drawing: 3.1)) great
5  G:   so have we got underneath slate
6        mountain
7  F:   .hh yep
8  G:   ye[ah]
9  F:      [so] we've got like a backwards
10       ee shape anyway
11 G:   so from
12 F:   for [the (X)]
13 G:       {[slate mou]n}₂{tain,
14 F:   [ya::h]
15 G:   [on the left}₃ {we] should we be
16       now on the left hand side of slate
17       mountain}₄
18 F:   on the left hand side
19 G:   yeah we should be:: {have come
20       round and underneath it}₅ (1.1)
21       god I can't reverse it {it's round
22       this side like this}₆
```

Figure 13 Second-person gesture

Prior to the example in Figure 13, F asked a question about the route G has been describing. Up until this point in the interaction, G and F have established a system where G is gesturing from F's perspective. On lines 1–3, G says 'then it goes back out (0.3) and it's gonna go back underneath slate mountain'. Accompanying her speech, G produces a gesture where her right hand depicts slate mountain and her left hand depicts the route that goes underneath it. This is unusual for two reasons. First, this type of gesture construction, where one hand is held to depict a stable object and the other hand moves to depict something interacting with the stable object, is typically realised with the dominant hand doing the moving and the non-dominant hand doing the holding (Enfield, 2009). However, G is right-handed, so this gesture is not what we would expect her to produce. The other unusual thing is based on G and F's system for representing gestures from F's perspective: G's gesture depicts the route as we (and F) see it on the map and not how she sees it.

On lines 15–16, G says 'on the left we should be now on the left-hand side of slate mountain'. However, on both occasions that she says 'left' she produces a gesture which, to the follower, depicts 'right'. This is at odds with the system G and F have established. In other words, to F she is gesturing 'right' and saying 'left'. This does not go unnoticed by F, who questions this use of 'left' on line 18. Then, F's question results in G abandoning the system, saying on lines 21–2: 'god I can't reverse it it's round this side like this'. So, G is clearly finding it difficult to maintain a different perspective from her own. When G abandons their system G does two things, one linguistically and one gesturally.

Linguistically she switches to deictic expressions ('this side', 'like this'). These expressions do not convey semantic information by themselves but invite a comprehender to use the spatial model to infer what G is talking about. Gesturally, G invites F to share her perspective by rotating her body and is now gesturing in a space where left and right are shared by both. What is happening here is that G is aligning the spatial model, the distal scene, the proximal scene and the base scene so that they are directly mapped onto each other. Once she does this, the role of the discourse model (in the sense of the lexical meaning) is reduced and she relies entirely on the spatial model. In other words, she appears to be trading the predictability of the discourse model for the predictability of the spatial model.

Further evidence for this can be found in the different spatial descriptions given in the example. Linguistically, the three spatial descriptions are quite different:

(20)   line 2: go back underneath

(21)   line 15: on the left

(22)   line 22: this side like this

From (20), it is underspecified whether 'back' refers to 'left' or 'right'. Presumably, F would be able to work this out based on the route discussed so far. The gesture G produces with (20) is not from her perspective but F's. However, since (20) does not encode directionality, there is no explicit mismatch (for G) between what they are saying and what they are gesturing. In (21), there is explicit reference to directionality, using the word 'left'. Here, G produces a gesture that also depicts leftness (from her perspective), resulting in F's confusion about the route. What I think is happening here is that the explicit mismatch between what G was expected to do (i.e., gesture left from F's perspective) and what she was going to say resulted in a mismatch between what she wanted to communicate and what she actually gestured. Once this mismatch is brought to G's attention, there is a breakdown of her adopting F's perspective. The result is that she shifts perspective so that both G and F share a perspective and she uses deictic expressions (which convey minimal semantic information) to describe the route, offloading the burden of communicating to her gesture. In other words, in response to the problems associated with mismatched language and gesture content, G produces an utterance in (22) in which the content of gesture dominates language.

This might seem like a one-off. However, Wilson and Argyriou (2019) analysed every instance of gesture from the map task data for the perspective a gesture was encoded in and found that a shared perspective was more likely to be adopted in response to a question about the route, than an initial description of a section of the route. What G is doing in this task is describing space. Language is not the best tool for describing space because language is structured compositionally rather than spatially. When language can no longer be predictably used to refer to space, gesture represents a better tool because it can be directly predicted using a spatial model. However, owing to the inherent inversion of a producer's base scene and the comprehender's representation of a distal scene, this creates a potential problem. That said, it is a problem that can be solved by bringing the distal scene and the base scene into alignment for both producer and comprehender.

4.4.2 Gesture-Framed Language

A recurrent finding in the literature was that gesture is redundantly fitted to language. This led to de Ruiter arguing for the AR-sketch model. While it is the case that gesture often follows the structure of speech (as demonstrated in Section 3), I have argued that this is not a necessary principle of gesture. Here, I want to argue that the tendency for gesture to follow language is based on the predictability of the communicative impact of speech.

Figure 14 shows F asking G whether they have understood part of the route. In lines 1–3, she says 'does the peak go over the top of the: (0.6) tri=your pyramid'. Here, F is asking about the route as it goes up and over the top of the pyramid, which as part of the task design is an unshared landmark. In the task, G has a pyramid and F has an old temple, which appear in an identical position. In other words, in the (visually present) distal scene, F can see an old temple but has to remember that G has a pyramid. This fact will reduce the predictability of what she wants to say because she is having to retrieve from memory what landmark G has. This can be seen in the hesitancy and the false start.

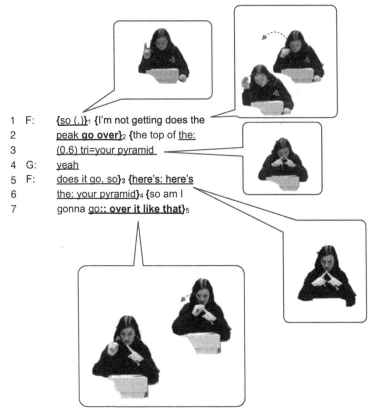

```
1  F:   {so (.)}₁ {I'm not getting does the
2       peak go over}₂ {the top of the:
3       (0.6) tri=your pyramid
4  G:   yeah
5  F:   does it go, so}₃ {here's: here's
6       the: your pyramid}₄ {so am I
7       gonna go:: over it like that}₅
```

Figure 14 Language and gesture–framed utterances

In fact, it appears that F is having some word-finding difficulties (she is finding it difficult to predict the lexical act 'pyramid') because she initially produces 'tri' (which is presumably going to be 'triangle') before saying 'pyramid'. As a word-finding gesture, which appears to facilitate F accessing the lexeme 'pyramid', G produces a gesture (which starts at the same time as the word 'top' and continues after she has finished her turn) depicting a triangle.

However, her gesturing starts before the search of the word 'pyramid'. The question 'does the peak go over the top of the pyramid' is accompanied by two gestures. The first depicts the way in which the route 'goes over' the pyramid and the second depicts the pyramid itself. I believe that the arrangement of these two gestures is not spatial or temporal; the route and the pyramid are not realised so that the route is travelling over the top of the pyramid, as gestured. What happens is that F starts describing the route going over and then produces a separate gesture, which is triggered by her inability to predict the lexical act 'pyramid'.

There are three key points to make about the speech and the gesture in lines 1–3. First, the route gesture is co-expressive with 'go over', and provides additional information since it depicts the direction the route takes over the pyramid. Second, there is no spatial relationship between the depicted route and the depicted pyramid. And third, the gesture follows the structure of the speech. In this turn, her language/gesture are exactly what would be expected according to a language architecture.

Linguistically, it makes most sense for the subject of the sentence to be the route (referred to here as 'the peak') and to predicate it with the verb phrase 'go over the top of the pyramid'. However, the thing that is being described spatially has the inverse spatial/temporal properties. The pyramid exists first and the route is drawn relative to it. Interestingly, when F elaborates on this sequence in lines 5–7, this is precisely how she describes it. Like her description in lines 1–3, F's description in lines 5–7 comprises two gestures. However, this time the order is reversed. First she depicts the pyramid then she depicts the route going over it. I believe that these two gestures are realised as a gesture sequence, where the second gesture is spatially and temporally linked to the first. Evidence for this comes from the fact that the left side of the triangle is held following the commencement of the depiction of the route, so that the relationship between the route gesture and the pyramid gesture is made explicit.

When we start to consider F's language, things become clearer still. She begins by saying 'here's: here's the: your pyramid'. Notice once again the hesitancy around the word 'pyramid'. Once again there is a shift from the definite article to the possessive pronoun. However, this time F uses the deictic expression 'here's' as a way to establish the triangle in front of her as an analogue for the pyramid on G's map. Once she has done this, the triangle in front of her and not the pyramid on G's map is the direct referent of her speech. In other words, F has established an analogue in the base scene (i.e., her gesture) for something in the distal scene (i.e., G's pyramid). In doing so, the 'it' in 'so am I gonna go:: over it like that' does not refer to G's pyramid but to her gesture. This avoids the issues surrounding the mismatch between what is on her map and what is on G's map, providing a stable (gestural) representation to make predictions about. However, there is something else here as well. The language is fitted to the gesture. The pyramid is introduced in a clause which establishes it and then the route is introduced in a subordinate clause (headed by 'so') which describes the route. Because language is linear and compositional, the only way to do this is with anaphoric expressions.

This example provides evidence that when an element that is to be packaged in speech is not highly predictable, such as when a referent needs to be retrieved from memory, gesture can be used as a more predictable foundation to structure an utterance. When this is the case, utterance producers create gesture-framed utterances. The reason why gesture framing is not the norm is that language, by its very nature is predictable over a greater range of contexts than gesture.

4.4.3 Summary

These two examples, I believe, demonstrate the utility of a predictability based understanding of why composite utterances are produced. Both of them suggest that when predicting lexical acts becomes difficult, gestures are used. From them I want to suggest three principles that appear to capture the way people compose their utterances (see Box 8).

Box 8 Principles of Utterance Composition

Producers aim to:

1. Produce the communicative act that has the most predictable communicative impact.
2. Avoid information mismatches across modalities.
3. Avoid mismatches between distal scene and base scene.

These principles capture typical characteristics in everyday interaction. Further, they explain why the structure of gesture is typically, but not necessarily, fitted to the structure of language. And they do so without being unconstrained or involving the need to match the information to be represented in language and gesture, which were de Ruiter's (2017, p. 66) objections to the interface hypothesis. They achieve this because both language and gesture are constrained by context (the discourse and the spatial models) and because there is a single underlying multimodal representation (or idea unit).

5 Conclusions

My goal in this Element has been to try to incorporate gesture into a pragmatic model of communication. The model of communication I have adopted treats utterances as evidence from which the reason the utterance was produced can be inferred. Following many working in pragmatics, I have argued that such inferences are facilitated by assuming a context that includes a discourse model a spatial model and a model of the utterance producer. Further, utterances are complex hierarchical actions with intended meanings at the top and actual behaviours produced at the bottom. I have argued that people are not necessarily aware of the behaviours they produce, but they may become aware when things do not go as predicted. This is key to understanding pragmatics because complex actions can be treated as conforming to hierarchical predictions. Utterance producers have intentions to inform and these intentions result in predictions of what to say, what grammatical constructions to produce, what words to produce and what sounds to make. If they work, there is no need to be aware of lower-level predictions. Furthermore, an utterance comprehender is using the same hierarchy and therefore similar predictions to work out what someone is trying to communicate.

Where does gesture fit into this? I have argued that the semantic structure from which what is said is derived is not linguistic in nature, but amodal. Utterances are based on idea units and language typically represents only certain aspects of an idea unit. The result is that language can be only indirectly predicted using a spatial model. Gesture, which is a spatial analogue, can be directly predicted using a spatial model. Therefore, when predicting an utterance becomes more difficult, such as when someone has privileged access to something or when they do not shared a spatial frame of reference, gesturing increases. However, when language does a good job of providing evidence for an informative intention, then the discourse model which includes the syntax of the language is used to make predictions and the structure of gesture appears to be fitted to the syntactic structure.

These ideas explain gesture without falling foul of two problematic assumptions from the pragmatics and the gesture literature. The first is that utterances require awareness of what is uttered. If we assume that utterance producers and comprehenders are aware of the informative content of an informative intention, then there is no need to be fully aware of how this was achieved so long as people act in a not unexpected way. Since I am assuming that both the linguistic and the gestural aspects of an utterance are produced to satisfy this informative intention, then there is no need for communicators to be aware of gesture either. Why, one might ask, does it seem like we are aware of language in a way that we are not perhaps aware of gesture? To this I would answer that language is a conventional system; therefore, its whole existence is determined by being remembered. Utterances are not merely tokens but tokens of types, and what we are usually aware of (if we are actually aware at all) are the types of thing we said, not the tokens. Representational gestures of the kind I have been focussing on are not tokens of types, and, perhaps as a result, we feel less aware of them.

The second problematic assumption relates to the information contained in both linguistic and gestural aspects of utterances. It seems that gesture often communicates 'the same' information as speech and therefore is redundant communicatively. I believe that this relies on a misunderstanding of how communication works and is solved by the notion of predictability argued for in this Element. If communication is about encoding information into different modalities (speech and gesture) and a comprehender understands an utterance when they decode the information presented, then any duplicated information would be redundant. However, that is a problematic conceptualisation of communication, as has long been recognised in pragmatics. Communication works because a producer presents evidence from which the reason that evidence was presented can be inferred. From this perspective, two sources of evidence that both point to the same conclusion are not redundant but degenerate. This is how gesture works. Gesture is not recruited simply because linguistic encoding is difficult; it is recruited because the difficulty of linguistic encoding makes it difficult to predict how well an utterance will realise an informative intention. However, this also means that gesture is recruited whenever it makes the prediction of how well an utterance will realise an information intention easier.

The final argument in the last paragraph implies that there is a predictive threshold for when people gesture. If predicting the realisation of an informative intention based on a discourse model becomes harder or if a spatial model is a better predictor, then people will produce more gesture. The implications of this are that gesturing is not likely to be a tool used in a universally predictable way; rather, different people and different cultures will gesture to varying degrees. I believe that understanding how this predictive threshold for gesture works should be the aim of future work in both pragmatics and gesture studies.

References

Alibali, M. W., Evans, J. L., Hostetter, A. B., Ryan, K., & Mainela-Arnold, E. (2009). Gesture–speech integration in narrative: Are children less redundant than adults? *Gesture*, *9*(3), 290–311.

Alibali, M. W., Kita, S., & Young, A. J. (2000). Gesture and the process of speech production: We think, therefore we gesture. *Language and Cognitive Processes*, *15*(6), 593–613.

Altmann, G. T., & Kamide, Y. (1999). Incremental interpretation at verbs: Restricting the domain of subsequent reference. *Cognition*, *73*(3), 247–64.

Austin, J. L. (1962). *How to do things with words*. Oxford: Clarendon Press. (Edited by James O. Urmson & Marina Sbisá.)

Bara, B. G. (2010). *Cognitive pragmatics: The mental processes of communication*. Cambridge, MA: MIT Press.

Bara, B. G. (2017). Cognitive pragmatics. In Y. Huang (Ed.), *The Oxford handbook of pragmatics* (pp. 279–99). New York: Oxford University Press.

Bara, B. G., Enrici, I., & Adenzato, M. (2016). At the core of pragmatics: The neural substrates of communicative intentions. In G. Hickok & S. L. Small (Eds.), *Neurobiology of language* (pp. 675–85). New York: Elsevier.

Barsalou, L. W. (1983). Ad hoc categories. *Memory and Cognition*, *11*(3), 211–27.

Barsalou, L. W. (1999). Perceptual symbol systems. *Behavioral and Brain Sciences*, *22*(4), 577–660.

Barsalou, L. W. (2008). Grounded cognition. *Annual Review of Psychology*, *59*, 617–45.

Bavelas, J., Gerwing, J., Sutton, C., & Prevost, D. (2008). Gesturing on the telephone: Independent effects of dialogue and visibility. *Journal of Memory and Language*, *58*(2), 495–520.

Bavelas, J., & Healing, S. (2013). Reconciling the effects of mutual visibility on gesturing: A review. *Gesture*, *13*(1), 63–92.

Beattie, G., & Shovelton, H. (1999a). Do iconic hand gestures really contribute anything to the semantic information conveyed by speech? An experimental investigation. *Semiotica*, *123*(1–2), 1–30.

Beattie, G., & Shovelton, H. (1999b). Mapping the range of information contained in the iconic hand gestures that accompany spontaneous speech. *Journal of Language and Social Psychology*, *18*(4), 438–62.

Beattie, G., & Shovelton, H. (2001). An experimental investigation of the role of different types of iconic gesture in communication: A semantic feature approach. *Gesture*, *1*(2), 129–49.

Beattie, G., & Shovelton, H. (2002). An experimental investigation of some properties of individual iconic gestures that mediate their communicative power. *British Journal of Psychology, 93*(2), 179–92.

Beattie, G., & Shovelton, H. (2006). When size really matters: How a single semantic feature is represented in the speech and gesture modalities. *Gesture, 6*(1), 63–84.

Cafazzo, S., Natoli, E., & Valsecchi, P. (2012). Scent-marking behaviour in a pack of free-ranging domestic dogs. *Ethology, 118*(10), 955–66.

Campisi, E., & Mazzone, M. (2016). Do people intend to gesture? A review of the role of intentionality in gesture production and comprehension. *Reti Saperi Linguaggi–Italian Journal of Cognitive Science, 3*(2), 285–300.

Campisi, E., & Özyürek, A. (2013). Iconicity as a communicative strategy: Recipient design in multimodal demonstrations for adults and children. *Journal of Pragmatics, 47*(1), 14–27.

Carston, R. (2002). *Thoughts and utterances: The pragmatics of explicit communication.* Oxford: Blackwell.

Carston, R. (2010). Xiii – Metaphor: Ad hoc concepts, literal meaning and mental images. In *Proceedings of the Aristotelian Society* (Vol. 110, pp. 295–321). Oxford: Oxford University Press.

Carston, R. (2018). Figurative language, mental imagery, and pragmatics. *Metaphor and Symbol, 33*(3), 198–217.

Chu, M., Meyer, A., Foulkes, L., & Kita, S. (2014). Individual differences in frequency and saliency of speech-accompanying gestures: The role of cognitive abilities and empathy. *Journal of Experimental Psychology: General, 143*(2), 694–709.

Clark, A. (2015). *Surfing uncertainty: Prediction, action, and the embodied mind.* Oxford: Oxford University Press.

Clark, H. H. (1996). *Using language.* Cambridge: Cambridge University Press.

Clark, H. H. (2016). Depicting as a method of communication. *Psychological Review, 123*(3), 324–47.

Clark, H. H., & Wilkes-Gibbs, D. (1986). Referring as a collaborative process. *Cognition, 22*(1), 1–39.

Cohen, D., Beattie, G., & Shovelton, H. (2011). Tracking the distribution of individual semantic features in gesture across spoken discourse: New perspectives in multi-modal interaction. *Semiotica, 185*(1–4), 147–88.

Cooperrider, K., Slotta, J., & Nunez, R. (2018). The preference for pointing with the hand is not universal. *Cognitive Science, 42*(4), 1375–90.

Davidson, D. (2001). *Essays on actions and events: Philosophical essays* (Vol. 1). Oxford: Oxford University Press.

Davies, C., & Richardson, A. (2021). Semantic as well as referential relevance facilitates the processing of referring expressions. *Journal of Pragmatics*, *178*(1), 258–69.

Degen, J., Hawkins, R. D., Graf, C., Kreiss, E., & Goodman, N. D. (2020). When redundancy is useful: A Bayesian approach to 'overinformative' referring expressions. *Psychological Review*, *127*(4), 591–621.

de Ruiter, J. P. (2000). The production of gesture and speech. In D. McNeill (Ed.), *Language and gesture* (pp. 284–311). Cambridge: Cambridge University Press.

de Ruiter, J. P. (2006). Can gesticulation help aphasic people speak, or rather, communicate? *International Journal of Speech-Language Pathology*, *8*(2), 124–7.

de Ruiter, J. P. (2007). Postcards from the mind: The relationship between speech, imagistic gesture, and thought. *Gesture*, *7*(1), 21–38.

de Ruiter, J. P. (2017). The asymmetric redundancy of gesture and speech. In R. B. Church, M. W. Alibali & S. D. Kelly (Eds.), *Why gesture? How the hands function in speaking, thinking and communicating* (pp. 59–76). Philadelphia, PA: John Benjamins.

de Ruiter, J. P., Bangerter, A., & Dings, P. (2012). The interplay between gesture and speech in the production of referring expressions: Investigating the tradeoff hypothesis. *Topics in Cognitive Science*, *4*(2), 232–48.

di Pellegrino, G., Fadiga, L., Fogassi, L., Gallese, V., & Rizzolatti, G. (1992). Understanding motor events: A neurophysiological study. *Experimental Brain Research*, *91*(1), 176–80.

Ekman, P. (1999). Emotional and conversational nonverbal signals. In L. S. Messing & R. Campbell (Eds.), *Gesture, speech, and sign* (pp. 45–55). Oxford: Oxford University Press.

Enfield, N. J. (2009). *The anatomy of meaning: Speech, gesture, and composite utterances*. Cambridge: Cambridge University Press.

Enfield, N. J. (2013). A 'composite utterances' approach to meaning. In C. Müller, A. Cienki, E. Fricke, S. Ladewig, D. McNeill & S. Teßendorf (Eds.), *Body – language – communication: An international handbook on multimodality in human interaction* (Vol. 1, pp. 689–706). Berlin: De Gruyter Mouton.

Enfield, N. J., & Sidnell, J. (2017). *The concept of action*. Cambridge: Cambridge University Press.

Enrici, I., Adenzato, M., Cappa, S., Bara, B. G., & Tettamanti, M. (2011). Intention processing in communication: A common brain network for language and gestures. *Journal of Cognitive Neuroscience*, *23*(9), 2415–31.

Enrici, I., Bara, B. G., & Adenzato, M. (2019). Theory of mind, pragmatics and the brain: Converging evidence for the role of intention processing as a core feature of human communication. *Pragmatics & Cognition, 26*(1), 5–38.

Fiengo, R. (2007). *Asking questions: Using meaningful structures to imply ignorance.* Oxford: Oxford University Press.

Gallagher, S. (2020). *Action and interaction.* Oxford: Oxford University Press.

Garrod, S., & Pickering, M. J. (2004). Why is conversation so easy? *Trends in Cognitive Sciences, 8*(1), 8–11.

Gerwing, J., & Bavelas, J. (2004). Linguistic influences on gesture's form. *Gesture, 4*(2), 157–95.

Geurts, B. (2019). What's wrong with gricean pragmatics. In *Exling 2019: Proceedings of the 10th international conference of experimental linguistics* (pp. 1–9). Athens: ExLing Society.

Goldin-Meadow, S., Nusbaum, H., Kelly, S. D., & Wagner, S. (2001). Explaining math: Gesturing lightens the load. *Psychological Science, 12*(6), 516–22.

Goodman, N. D., & Frank, M. C. (2016). Pragmatic language interpretation as probabilistic inference. *Trends in Cognitive Sciences, 20*(11), 818–29.

Grice, H. P. (1957). Meaning. *Philosophical Review, 66*(3), 377–88.

Grice, H. P. (1968). Utterer's meaning, sentence-meaning and word-meaning. *Foundations of Language, 4*, 1–18.

Grice, H. P. (1975). Logic and conversation. In P. Cole & J. L. Morgan (Eds.), *Syntax and semantics 3: Speech acts* (pp. 41–58). New York: Academic Press.

Grice, H. P. (1989). *Studies in the way of words.* Cambridge, MA: Harvard University Press.

Gsell, A., Innes, J., de Monchy, P., & Brunton, D. (2010). The success of using trained dogs to locate sparse rodents in pest-free sanctuaries. *Wildlife Research, 37*(1), 39–46.

Harman, G. H. (1965). The inference to the best explanation. *Philosophical Review, 74*(1), 88–95.

Hart, B. L. (1974). Environmental and hormonal influences on urine marking behavior in the adult male dog. *Behavioral Biology, 11*(2), 167–76.

Hauser, M. D. (1996). *The evolution of communication.* Cambridge, MA: MIT Press.

Heyes, C. M. (2018). *Cognitive gadgets: The cultural evolution of thinking.* Cambridge, MA: Harvard University Press.

Heyes, C. M., & Catmur, C. (2020). What happened to mirror neurons? *Perspectives on Psychological Science, 17*(1), 153–68.

Heyes, C. M., & Frith, C. D. (2014). The cultural evolution of mind reading. *Science, 344*(6190), 1243091.

Hohwy, J. (2013). *The predictive mind.* Oxford: Oxford University Press.

Holler, J., & Bavelas, J. (2017). Multi-modal communication of common ground: A review of social functions. In S. D. Kelly, R. Breckinridge Church, & M. W. Alibali (Eds.), *Why gesture? How the hands function in speaking, thinking and communicating* (pp. 213–240). Philadelphia, PA: John Benjamins.

Holler, J., & Beattie, G. (2002). A micro-analytic investigation of how iconic gestures and speech represent core semantic features in talk. *Semiotica, 142*(1/4), 31–70.

Holler, J., & Beattie, G. (2003). Pragmatic aspects of representational gestures: Do speakers use them to clarify verbal ambiguity for the listener? *Gesture, 3*(2), 127–54.

Holler, J., Schubotz, L., Kelly, S. D., Hagoort, P., Schuetze, M., & Özyürek, A. (2014). Social eye gaze modulates processing of speech and co-speech gesture. *Cognition, 133*(3), 692–7.

Horn, L. (2004). Implicature. In L. Horn & G. Ward (Eds.), *The handbook of pragmatics* (pp. 3–28). Oxford: Blackwell Publishing.

Hostetter, A. B., & Alibali, M. W. (2007). Raise your hand if you're spatial: Relations between verbal and spatial skills and gesture production. *Gesture, 7*(1), 73–95.

Hostetter, A. B., Alibali, M. W., & Kita, S. (2007). I see it in my hands' eye: Representational gestures reflect conceptual demands. *Language and Cognitive Processes, 22*(3), 313–36.

Iverson, J. M., & Goldin-Meadow, S. (2001). The resilience of gesture in talk: Gesture in blind speakers and listeners. *Developmental Science, 4*(4), 416–22.

Iverson, J. M., Tencer, H. L., Lany, J., & Goldin-Meadow, S. (2000). The relation between gesture and speech in congenitally blind and sighted language-learners. *Journal of Nonverbal Behavior, 24*(2), 105–30.

Kelly, S. D., Barr, D. J., Church, R. B., & Lynch, K. (1999). Offering a hand to pragmatic understanding: The role of speech and gesture in comprehension and memory. *Journal of Memory and Language, 40*(4), 577–92.

Kelly, S. D., Healey, M., Özyürek, A., & Holler, J. (2015). The processing of speech, gesture, and action during language comprehension. *Psychonomic Bulletin & Review, 22*(2), 517–23.

Kelly, S. D., Kravitz, C., & Hopkins, M. (2004). Neural correlates of bimodal speech and gesture comprehension. *Brain and Language, 89*(1), 253–60.

Kelly, S. D., Özyürek, A., & Maris, E. (2010). Two sides of the same coin: Speech and gesture mutually interact to enhance comprehension. *Psychological Science, 21*(2), 260–7.

Kendon, A. (1980). Gesticulation and speech: Two aspects of the process of utterance. In M. Ritchie Key (Ed.), *The relationship of verbal and nonverbal communication* (Vol. 25, pp. 207–27). The Hague: Mouton Publishers.

Kendon, A. (2004). *Gesture: Visible action as utterance*. Cambridge: Cambridge University Press.

Kenny, A. J. (1966). Practical inference. *Analysis, 26*(3), 65–75.

Kepa, K., & Perry, J. (2020). Pragmatics. In E. N. Zalta & U. Nodelman (Eds.), *The Standford encyclopedia of philosophy*. Stanford, CA: Stanford University.

Kissine, M. (2013). *From utterances to speech acts*. Cambridge: Cambridge University Press.

Kita, S. (2009). Cross-cultural variation of speech-accompanying gesture: A review. *Language and Cognitive Processes, 24*(2), 145–67.

Kita, S., & Davies, T. S. (2009). Competing conceptual representations trigger co-speech representational gestures. *Language and Cognitive Processes, 24*(5), 761–75.

Kita, S., & Özyürek, A. (2003). What does cross-linguistic variation in semantic coordination of speech and gesture reveal? Evidence for an interface representation of spatial thinking and speaking. *Journal of Memory and Language, 48*(1), 16–32.

Kita, S., Özyürek, A., Allen, S., Brown, A., Furman, R., & Ishizuka, T. (2007). Relations between syntactic encoding and co-speech gestures: Implications for a model of speech and gesture production. *Language and Cognitive Processes, 22*(8), 1212–36.

Kobayashi, H., & Kohshima, S. (2001). Unique morphology of the human eye and its adaptive meaning: Comparative studies on external morphology of the primate eye. *Journal of Human Evolution, 40*(5), 419–35.

Kockelman, P. (2012). Meaning, motivation, and mind: Some conditions and consequences for the flexibility and intersubjectivity of cognitive processes. *New Ideas in Psychology, 30*(1), 65–85.

Kokocińska-Kusiak, A., Woszczyło, M., Zybala, M., Maciocha, J., Barłowska, K., & Dzięcioł, M. (2021). Canine olfaction: Physiology, behavior, and possibilities for practical applications. *Animals, 11*(8), 2463.

Krauss, R. M., Chen, Y., & Gottesmamn, R. F. (2000). Lexical gestures and lexical access: A process model. In D. McNeill (Ed.), *Language and gesture* (Vol. 2, pp. 261–83). Cambridge: Cambridge University Press.

Krauss, R. M., Dushay, R. A., Chen, Y., & Rauscher, F. (1995). The communicative value of conversational hand gesture. *Journal of Experimental Social Psychology, 31*(6), 533–52.

Levelt, W. J. (1993). *Speaking: From intention to articulation* (Vol. 1). Cambridge, MA: MIT Press.

Levinson, S. C. (1979). Activity types and language. *Linguistics*, *17*(5–6), 365–400.

Levinson, S. C. (1995). Interactional biases in human thinking. In E. N. Goody (Ed.), *Social intelligence and interaction* (pp. 221–60). Cambridge: Cambridge University Press.

Levinson, S. C. (2000). *Presumptive meanings: The theory of generalized conversational implicature*. Cambridge, MA: MIT Press.

Levinson, S. C. (2012). Action formation and ascription. In J. Sidnell & T. Stivers (Eds.), *The handbook of conversation analysis* (pp. 101–30). Chichester: John Wiley & Sons.

Lewis, D. (1969). *Convention: A philosophical study*. Cambridge, MA: Harvard University Press.

Liszkowski, U., Brown, P., Callaghan, T., Takada, A., & de Vos, C. (2012). A prelinguistic gestural universal of human communication. *Cognitive Science*, *36*(4), 698–713.

Mason, P. H., Domínguez D., J. F., Winter, B., & Grignolio, A. (2015). Hidden in plain view: Degeneracy in complex systems. *Biosystems*, *128*, 1–8.

Mazzone, M., & Campisi, E. (2013). Distributed intentionality: A model of intentional behavior in humans. *Philosophical Psychology*, *26*(2), 267–90.

McGuire, B., & Bemis, K. E. (2017). Scent marking in shelter dogs: Effects of body size. *Applied Animal Behaviour Science*, *186*, 49–55.

McGuire, J. T., & Kable, J. W. (2012). Decision makers calibrate behavioral persistence on the basis of time-interval experience. *Cognition*, *124*(2), 216–26.

McNeill, D. (1992). *Hand and mind: What gestures reveal about thought*. Chicago, IL: University of Chicago Press.

McNeill, D. (2000). Introduction. In D. McNeill (Ed.), *Language and gesture* (pp. 1–12). Cambridge: Cambridge University Press.

McNeill, D. (2005). *Gesture and thought*. London: University of Chicago Press.

McNeill, D. (2012). *How language began: Gesture and speech in human evolution*. Cambridge: Cambridge University Press.

McNeill, D. (2015). *Why we gesture: The surprising role of hand movements in communication*. Cambridge: Cambridge University Press.

Melinger, A., & Levelt, W. J. (2004). Gesture and the communicative intention of the speaker. *Gesture*, *4*(2), 119–41.

Millikan, R. G. (1984). *Language, thought, and other biological categories: New foundations for realism*. Cambridge, MA: MIT Press.

Moore, R. (2017). Gricean communication and cognitive development. *Philosophical Quarterly*, *67*(267), 303–26.

Morsella, E., & Krauss, R. M. (2004). The role of gestures in spatial working memory and speech. *American Journal of Psychology*, *117*(3), 411–24.

Neale, S. (1992). Paul Grice and the philosophy of language. *Linguistics and Philosophy*, *15*, 509–59.

Noordzij, M., Newman-Norlund, S., De Ruiter, J. P., Hagoort, P., Levinson, S., & Toni, I. (2009). Brain mechanisms underlying human communication. *Frontiers in Human Neuroscience*, *3*, 14.

Novack, M. A., Wakefield, E. M., & Goldin-Meadow, S. (2016). What makes a movement a gesture? *Cognition*, *146*, 339–48.

Ozcaliskan, S., Lucero, C., & Goldin-Meadow, S. (2016). Does language shape silent gesture? *Cognition*, *148*, 10–18.

Özyürek, A. (2002). Do speakers design their cospeech gestures for their addressees? The effects of addressee location on representational gestures. *Journal of Memory and Language*, *46*(4), 688–704.

Özyürek, A. (2014). Hearing and seeing meaning in speech and gesture: Insights from brain and behaviour. *Philosophical Transactions of the Royal Society B: Biological Sciences*, *369*(1651), 20130296.

Özyürek, A., Kita, S., Allen, S., Furman, R., & Brown, A. (2005). How does linguistic framing of events influence co-speech gestures? Insights from crosslinguistic variations and similarities. *Gesture*, *5*(1–2), 219–40.

Özyürek, A., Willems, R. M., Kita, S., & Hagoort, P. (2007). On-line integration of semantic information from speech and gesture: Insights from event-related brain potentials. *Journal of Cognitive Neuroscience*, *19*(4), 605–16.

Parikh, P. (2019). *Communication and content* (Vol. Topics at the Grammar-Discourse Interface) (No. 4). Berlin: Language Science Press.

Pearl, J., & Mackenzie, D. (2018). *The book of why: The new science of cause and effect*. New York: Basic Books.

Peirce, C. S. (1998). *The essential Peirce: Selected philosophical writings, 1893–1913* (Vol. 1). Bloomington: Indiana University Press.

Pickering, M. J., & Gambi, C. (2018). Predicting while comprehending language: A theory and review. *Psychological Bulletin*, *144*(10), 1002–44.

Pickering, M. J., & Garrod, S. (2007). Do people use language production to make predictions during comprehension? *Trends in Cognitive Sciences*, *11*(3), 105–10.

Pickering, M. J., & Garrod, S. (2013). An integrated theory of language production and comprehension. *Behavioral and Brain Sciences*, *36*(4), 329–47.

Proverbio, A. M., Gabaro, V., Orlandi, A., & Zani, A. (2015). Semantic brain areas are involved in gesture comprehension: An electrical neuroimaging study. *Brain and Language, 147*, 30–40.

Rauscher, F. H., Krauss, R. M., & Chen, Y. S. (1996). Gesture, speech, and lexical access: The role of lexical movements in speech production. *Psychological Science, 7*(4), 226–31.

Redcay, E., Velnoskey, K. R., & Rowe, M. L. (2016). Perceived communicative intent in gesture and language modulates the superior temporal sulcus. *Human Brain Mapping, 37*(10), 3444–61.

Rizzolatti, G., & Arbib, M. A. (1998). Language within our grasp. *Trends in Neurosciences, 21*(5), 188–94.

Rubio-Fernández, P. (2016). How redundant are redundant color adjectives? An efficiency-based analysis of color overspecification. *Frontiers in Psychology, 7*, 153.

Rubio-Fernández, P. (2019). Overinformative speakers are cooperative: Revisiting the Gricean maxim of quantity. *Cognitive Science, 43*(11), 12797.

Schiffer, S. (1972). *Meaning*. Oxford: Oxford University Press.

Searle, J. R. (1969). *Speech acts: An essay in the philosophy of language*. Cambridge: Cambridge University Press.

Searle, J. R. (1983). *Intentionality: An essay in the philosophy of mind*. Cambridge: Cambridge University Press.

Searle, J. R. (2010). *Making the social world: The structure of human civilization*. Oxford: Oxford University Press.

Sedivy, J., Tanenhaus, M., Chambers, C., & Carlson, G. (1999). Achieving incremental semantic interpretation through contextual representation. *Cognition, 71*(2), 109–47.

Shannon, C. E., & Weaver, W. (1949). *The mathematical theory of communication*. Urbana: University of Illinois Press.

Slobin, D. I. (1987). Thinking for speaking. *Annual Meeting of the Berkeley Linguistics Society, 13*, 435–45.

So, W. C., Alvan, Y. F., Yap, D. F., Kheng, E., & Yap, J. M. (2013). Iconic gestures prime words: Comparison of priming effects when gestures are presented alone and when they are accompanying speech. *Frontiers in Psychology, 4*, 779.

So, W. C., Kita, S., & Goldin-Meadow, S. (2009). Using the hands to identify who does what to whom: Gesture and speech go hand-in-hand. *Cognitive Science, 33*(1), 115–25.

Sperber, D. (1995). How do we communicate? In J Brockman & K. Matson (Eds.), *How things are: A science toolkit for the mind* (pp. 191–99). New York: Morrow.

Sperber, D., & Wilson, D. (1995). *Relevance: Communication and cognition* (2nd ed.). Oxford: Blackwell Publishing.

Sperber, D., & Wilson, D. (2002). Pragmatics, modularity and mind-reading. *Mind & Language, 17*(1–2), 3–23.

Spunt, R. P., Kemmerer, D., & Adolphs, R. (2016). The neural basis of conceptualizing the same action at different levels of abstraction. *Social Cognitive and Affective Neuroscience, 11*(7), 1141–51.

Spunt, R. P., Satpute, A. B., & Lieberman, M. D. (2011). Identifying the what, why, and how of an observed action: An fMRI study of mentalizing and mechanizing during action observation. *Journal of Cognitive Neuroscience, 23*(1), 63–74.

Stalnaker, R. C. (2002). Common ground. *Linguistics and Philosophy, 25,* 701–21.

Stenning, K., Lascarides, A., & Calder, J. (2006). *Introduction to cognition and communication.* Cambridge, MA: MIT Press.

Straube, B., Green, A., Weis, S., & Kircher, T. (2012, 11). A supramodal neural network for speech and gesture semantics: An fMRI study. *PLoS ONE, 7*(11), 1–10.

Talmy, L. (1985). Lexicalization patterns: Semantic structure in lexical forms. *Language Typology and Syntactic Description, 3*(99), 36–149.

Thesen, A., Steen, J. B., & Doving, K. B. (1993). Behaviour of dogs during olfactory tracking. *Journal of Experimental Biology, 180*(1), 247–51.

Tomasello, M. (2006). Why don't apes point? In N. Enfield & S. C. Levinson (Eds.), *The roots of human sociality: Culture, cognition and interaction* (pp. 506–24). Oxford: Berg.

Tomasello, M. (2010). *Origins of human communication.* Cambridge, MA: MIT Press.

Trujillo, J. P., Simanova, I., Bekkering, H., & Özyürek, A. (2018). Communicative intent modulates production and comprehension of actions and gestures: A kinect study. *Cognition, 180,* 38–51.

Trujillo, J. P., Simanova, I., Özyürek, A., & Bekkering, H. (2019). Seeing the unexpected: How brains read communicative intent through kinematics. *Cerebral Cortex, 30*(3), 1056–67.

Van Overwalle, F., & Baetens, K. (2009). Understanding others' actions and goals by mirror and mentalizing systems: A meta-analysis. *NeuroImage, 48*(3), 564–84.

Wagner, S. M., Nusbaum, H., & Goldin-Meadow, S. (2004). Probing the mental representation of gesture: Is handwaving spatial? *Journal of Memory and Language, 50*(4), 395–407.

Wesp, R., Hesse, J., Keutmann, D., & Wheaton, K. (2001). Gestures maintain spatial imagery. *American Journal of Psychology, 114*(4), 591–600.

Wharton, T. (2009). *Pragmatics and non-verbal communication.* Cambridge: Cambridge University Press.

Willems, R. M., Öyürek, A., & Hagoort, P. (2007). When language meets action: The neural integration of gesture and speech. *Cerebral Cortex, 17*(10), 2322–33.

Willems, R. M., Özyürek, A., & Hagoort, P. (2009). Differential roles for left inferior frontal and superior temporal cortex in multimodal integration of action and language. *NeuroImage, 47*(4), 1992–2004.

Willems, R. M., & Varley, R. (2010). Neural insights into the relation between language and communication. *Frontiers in Human Neuroscience, 4*, 203.

Wilson, D., & Wharton, T. (2006). Relevance and prosody. *Journal of Pragmatics, 38*(10), 1559–79.

Wilson, J. (2016). What co-speech gestures do: Investigating the role of visual behaviour accompanying language use during reference in interaction (unpublished doctoral dissertation). University of Leeds.

Wilson, J., & Argyriou, P. (2019, June). *When do speakers share gesture perspective?* Poster presented at Body up: Current trends and future directions in embodiment and social interaction.

Winter, B. (2014). Spoken language achieves robustness and evolvability by exploiting degeneracy and neutrality. *BioEssays, 36*(10), 960–7.

Wu, Y. C., & Coulson, S. (2005). Meaningful gestures: Electrophysiological indices of iconic gesture comprehension. *Psychophysiology, 42*(6), 654–67.

Wu, Y. C., & Coulson, S. (2007). Iconic gestures prime related concepts: An ERP study. *Psychonomic Bulletin & Review, 14*(1), 57–63.

Xu, J., Gannon, P. J., Emmorey, K., Smith, J. F., & Braun, A. R. (2009). Symbolic gestures and spoken language are processed by a common neural system. *Proceedings of the National Academy of Sciences, 106*(49), 20664–9.

Yorzinski, J. L., & Miller, J. (2020). Sclera color enhances gaze perception in humans. *PLoS ONE, 15*(2), e0228275.

Cambridge Elements

Pragmatics

Jonathan Culpeper

Lancaster University, UK

Jonathan Culpeper is Professor of English Language and Linguistics in the Department of Linguistics and English Language at Lancaster University, UK. A former co-editor-in-chief of the *Journal of Pragmatics* (2009–14), with research spanning multiple areas within pragmatics, his major publications include: *Impoliteness: Using Language to Cause Offence* (2011, CUP) and *Pragmatics and the English Language* (2014, Palgrave; with Michael Haugh).

Michael Haugh

University of Queensland, Australia

Michael Haugh is Professor of Linguistics and Applied Linguistics in the School of Languages and Cultures at the University of Queensland, Australia. A former co-editor-in-chief of the *Journal of Pragmatics* (2015–2020), with research spanning multiple areas within pragmatics, his major publications include: *Understanding Politeness* (2013, CUP; with Dániel Kádár), *Pragmatics and the English Language* (2014, Palgrave; with Jonathan Culpeper), and *Im/politeness Implicatures* (2015, Mouton de Gruyter).

About the Series

The Cambridge Elements in Pragmatics series showcases dynamic and high-quality original, concise and accessible scholarly works. Written for a broad pragmatics readership it encourages dialogue across different perspectives on language use. It is a forum for cutting-edge work in pragmatics: consolidating theory (especially through cross-fertilization), leading the development of new methods, and advancing innovative topics in pragmatics.

Cambridge Elements $\equiv$

Pragmatics

Elements in the Series

.

Printed in the United States
by Baker & Taylor Publisher Services